Jottings

a teacher's logbook

by Peter Jailall

Writing at the foot of the Pakaraima Mountains

Jottings
A Teacher's Logbook
by Peter Jailall

Published by: In Our Words Inc./www.inourwords.ca

Editor: Sabi Jailall

Book design: Shirley Aguinaldo

Library and Archives Canada Cataloguing in Publication

Jailall, Peter, 1944-, author

    Jottings: a teacher's logbook / Peter Jailall ;

introduction by Dr. Jim Cummins, OISE, University of Toronto.

ISBN 978-1-926926-36-0 (pbk.)

    1. Education. I. Title.

LB41.J34 2014   370   C2013-907619-0

Copyright ©2014 Peter Jailall

All rights reserved by the author who is solely responsible for the content. With the exception of brief quotes citing author credit, this work is covered by the copyright herein, and may not be reproduced without the prior permission of the copyright owner.

Dedication

For Sabi —
my wife, my colleague,
my editor and my friend.

Peter and Sabi, landing at Moruca

Contents

- 6   INTRODUCTION by Jim Cummins
- 7   PREFACE

- 9   DIALOGUES Conversations about Education
    - 10   Message from Mike Harmer
    - 11   The Writing-Led Curriculum
    - 13   Public Education
    - 15   Discipline
    - 17   Literacy in Our Schools
    - 19   Syntax Error
    - 21   Multicultural Education
    - 23   Women in Education

- 25   MONOLOGUES Concerning Education
    - 26   Message from Ernie Kuechmeister
    - 27   Radwanski Reviewed
    - 29   Teacher Bashing
    - 30   "No Minister!"
    - 32   Creating A Crisis
    - 34   Troubled Times
    - 36   '…we better pray"
    - 38   Talking Back
    - 40   E.Q.A.O.
    - 42   Children's Rights
    - 44   One Profession
    - 45   Labour of Love
    - 47   Teaching in the New Mainstream

49	The Gulf War
51	Whole-Language and Multiculturalism in Grades One and Two
63	Building Collegiality Through Storytelling
65	Writing Empowers ESL/ESD Learners: Case of Winnie (Age 6)
67	Suffer the Little Children
69	T'is the Season
71	Our Father …?
73	Stop Youth Bashing and Victim Blaming!
75	Recipe for a Good Trustee
77	Voting For Marginalized Students
79	Farewell
81	It's Not Easy

83 TRAVELOGUES Giving Back

84	Guyanese Children Living Under a Dictatorship
90	Going Outside
93	Guyana
95	Celebrating World Teachers' Day in Guyana
97	Working Holiday
99	Learning from the Natural Environment
102	Children of Mabaruma
103	Reflections on Volunteering Three Weeks in Mabaruma, Guyana
105	Teaching in Guyana
106	Guyana's Future Stunted by Shortage of Trained Teachers
108	Educator Urges Ongoing Training for Teachers — Impressed with Hinterland Children
110	When Two Tigers Killed Our Dogs
112	Teaching in Bartica
117	Using the Guyanese Language (Creolese) to teach Standard English

Introduction

In the pages of this generously vibrant book, Peter Jailall is described by the *Guyana Times* as "a teacher, poet, storyteller and an avid supporter of human rights, education, social justice and environmental protection" and by the children of Mabaruma as "the funny, friendly ole man." To me, Peter is friend, colleague, teacher, and the embodiment of inspirational education. A clarity of vision and generosity of spirit shines through his pedagogy whether it is practiced in remote corners of Guyana or in the comparatively privileged classrooms of Canada's largest urban area.

Peter's "jottings" span a 30-year period from the mid-1980s to the present time and yet they speak directly to the fundamental questions that educators today, in Canada and internationally, ask themselves, implicitly or explicitly, every time they enter a classroom. These questions include the following: *What am I doing here—what is my identity as an educator? What are my aspirations for the students I am teaching—what do I hope for them as a result of the time they are spending with me? How can I best connect with their experience so that they develop literacy and other academic skills and at the same time become confident people and responsible citizens?*

All instruction implies an image of the student and Peter is explicit about the image of the student implied by his teaching. In response to a question from Mike Harmer about what kind of graduates we should be striving to produce, Peter responds: "Young people able to think creatively and independently, exercise self-sufficiency, respect our democratic way of life and religious and cultural co-existence, be responsible for their own behaviour and sensitive to the needs and plights of others."

Fundamental to realizing this image of the student is an orientation to education that is infused with respect for students and their communities. Students' cultural experiences, languages, and religious beliefs represent the identities they bring to the classroom and our role as educators is to expand the personal, intellectual and academic possibilities ready to blossom within these identities. Expressed differently: *If we want students to emerge from 12 years of schooling as intelligent, imaginative, and linguistically talented, then we must treat them as intelligent, imaginative and linguistically talented from the day they walk into our classrooms.*

The essence of the pedagogical deep structure that emerges from Peter's jottings, the writing of his students, and the dialogue he enters into with us, his readers and colleagues, can be summarized in two powerful statements.

Human relationships are at the heart of schooling. Peter points out that when a child's full citizenship in the classroom community is not validated enthusiastically by the teacher he or she is likely to emerge from schooling with a poor self-concept, low academic achievement, and even deviant behavior. An example, in the Guyanese context is the frequent communication to students that their home language is deficient and unsuitable for education. Peter's response is that Creole is part of the children's soul and can be used very effectively to teach standard English. Instead of prohibiting Creole, teachers should communicate that each language has its place and children should be taught "to keep Standard English in their back pockets and pull it out when it is necessary."

Writing is a path to student empowerment. Although approaches to literacy instruction such as process writing and whole language have fallen out of fashion in recent years, there is an immense amount of research, large-scale and small-scale, quantitative and qualitative, that documents the central role of literacy engagement in the development of literacy skills. No less an institution than the Organisation for Economic Cooperation and Development (OECD) has documented over multiple large-scale international studies that literacy engagement is a stronger predictor of students' reading achievement than socioeconomic status. Peter's classrooms in both Canada and Guyana were hives of literacy engagement. Students listened to stories, read books, and above all wrote extensively on a daily basis for 45-60 minutes. The following passage, from Peter's article with Robert P. Parker on whole-language and multiculturalism, is worth quoting in its entirety because it speaks so clearly to the power of writing in a multicultural classroom:

Every child wrote something during that time, regardless of ability or interest. All wrote about whatever they wanted to, or were able to, using their available linguistic resources. Many returned to their writing at times during the day when they weren't engaged in other work. Some took their writing to the schoolyard at recess; some wrote on the school bus; and some wrote at home, alone or in collaboration with siblings, parents, relatives, or peers. Some children got together on weekends to play and spent some of their time writing. So, while "writing workshop" occurred officially each morning in Peter's classroom, it also occurred unofficially at many other times and in many other places.

Empowerment can be defined as "the collaborative creation of power." The more power that is generated by one partner in a relationship (personal or instructional), the more is available to be shared with the other partner. Writing, or the creation of what colleagues and I have called *identity texts*, develops not only literacy skills but also fuels empowerment. The products of students' writing, when shared with significant others (peers, parents, teachers), hold a mirror up to students in which their personal and academic identities are reflected back in a positive light. As Peter's instruction over many years illustrates, this fuels further literacy engagement.

Thank you Peter for sharing your jottings with us. Educational theorists and practitioners such as John Dewey in the United States, Célestin Freinet in France, and Sylvia Ashton-Warner in New Zealand have, over the past century, highlighted similar themes to those embedded in your pedagogy, particularly the centrality of students' experience, respect for children and communities, and the importance of self-expression through writing. However, none have communicated with the directness, passion and humanity expressed in these pages and in the classrooms you have taught in over many years.

Jim Cummins, Toronto, July 2014

Preface

I write daily in my journal keeping a record of my life. Through writing, I have conversations with myself about what I learn and what I need to know. I encourage students to keep their own journals and I continue to build collegiality with teachers as we continuously engage in conversations about education and classroom practices.

This book is a collection of my thoughts and ideas about teaching and learning since I began my career in 1963. It gives me great pleasure to share 'JOTTINGS.' I have been privileged and honoured to meet and teach with colleagues while volunteering with VSO/CUSO. I would like to thank the international team of teachers with whom I worked over the years.

Thanks to:

Kane Summerhayes, Vern Healey—from Australia.

Derek & Trudy Lovel, Ian Fennel, Shelly Dixon, Paul Warrel and Ian Scott—from the U.K.

Robert Parker from the U.S.A.

Teacher Shelly, teacher Anna from Holland, Teacher Raquel Cohelo from Portugal

Bharat Mathoo, Robin and Bejai Narayan, Michael Harmer, Ernie Keuchmeister, Robert McCallum and Leon Thompson from Canada.

Ian McDonald, Judaman Seecoomar, Joyce Trotman from Guyana

Franklin Harvey—Caribbean

I thank my family Sabi, Nari, Dave and Anjni Jailall.

A special thanks to Anjni for spending days on the computer preparing the manuscript; and to Robert McCallum for organizing the chapters.

Peter Jailall, July 29, 2014

Dialogues

Conversations about Education

Sabi in discussion with teachers at Anna Regina, Guyana

Message from Mike Harmer

I first came to know my remarkable friend Peter Jailall in the mid-1980s as the subject of an article in *The Appeel*, a newspaper published by and for the teachers of the then Peel Board of Education – a worthy journal on whose editorial board I represented the elementary staff.

The writer had quizzed Peter about his primary classroom in Malton and had come away extolling his innovative approach to student language learning, particularly written and spoken expression, and his views on multicultural education and children's rights.

Little did I know that I would soon be meeting Peter in person. He had recently returned from a year's professional development leave at the University of British Columbia studying multicultural education with Jack Kehoe, renowned professor of social and educational studies. Seeking a way to share his new perceptions and insights with colleagues, he was referred to me to enquire about the possibility of contributing to the newspaper on a regular basis.

The resulting happy association with *The Appeel*, and later with the elementary teachers' own publication, *The Beacon*, continued without interruption until Peter's retirement in 1998.

The column was to address contemporary issues in public education, both the immediate concerns of the teacher in the classroom (the students, and how best to meet their needs) and the wider concerns about decision-making and future directions at the Board, the Ministry and the Legislature.

In planning the column, Peter asked that it be shaped as a dialogue between the two of us: I was to ply him with questions and my occasional "two cents' worth" on a topic of the day, and he would respond. In the event, it proved a comfortable and productive format, less an interview than a conversation. And comments from the readership, whether dealing praise, taking issue or asking for advice, suggested a healthy approval rating.

Revisiting these conversations thirty years later only confirms for me the improbable scope of Peter's interests and expertise, his creativity, his commitment to the belief that everyone has the right to a quality education … truly a lifelong learner, lifelong teacher, lifelong humanitarian.

The Writing-Led Curriculum

With Peter Jailall (PJ) and Mike Harmer (MH)

(*The Appeel*, January-February 1986)

Mike Harmer (MH) continues his conversation with published author and primary teacher, at McBride Avenue P.S., Peter Jailall.

MH: Can you explain what you mean by a "writing-led curriculum?"

PJ: I mean writing used as an active learning process in the classroom to clarify meaning and to extend knowledge into different curriculum content areas. I do not think we can confine writing to just "the language arts." I feel that writing has a larger function in the total learning process. For example, writing can be used effectively in mathematics to encourage children to create their own problems and to find solutions to them. In science, writing plays a crucial role in recording results of experiments and observations.

MH: Why has so much emphasis been placed on writing recently?

PJ: Extensive research, done during the past decade by linguists and educators, reveals the close relationship between writing and learning and clarifies for us some old myths about how children learn language. Writing is a natural learning process which helps children in their development as persons. When writing, children make meaning and they make text into context. For some children writing can lead to a breakthrough in learning.

MH: Is writing more important than reading, speaking or listening?

PJ: It is difficult to give a yes or no answer. An integrated use of all four processes is the ideal and should be pursued by teachers whenever possible. But I must point out that teachers and researchers have neglected writing for a long time. More time, effort and money have been allocated to the study of reading, listening and speaking. Also, these aspects of literacy have been around for a long time in human societies, especially spoken language. Writing has been neglected, partly because it is a difficult process and partly because of our lack of knowledge of the process. Writing is a process that integrates thought in a very efficient manner. Writing, like life itself, is an ongoing process.

MH: What can teachers do to help children to become writers?

PJ: It is important that teachers themselves engage in writing in order to experience the complexity of the process. There is no do-it-by-number approach in getting children to become competent writers and learners. The child must be allowed to demonstrate what he/she knows about language before the teacher passes judgement. Teachers of young children should avoid treating their charges as "literacy orphans" and empty vessels.

Children know a lot about language before they come to school. The observant language professional will draw upon that knowledge. A language learning classroom is one that Jerome Harste describes as an "open entry environment" in which children are allowed to learn in a risk-free language setting, where teacher and pupils have the opportunity to create language and to use language without constraints.

MH: How easy is it to turn a child off writing?

PJ: It is very easy, but teachers turned on to writing themselves are less likely to turn children off. Most children will become reluctant writers if they are not given enough time and opportunities for writing and if they do not have easy access to writing materials. Children will be turned off if they perceive that teachers are more interested in cosmetic surface structure than in content. They will hesitate if their errors are seen as "carelessness" and not as necessary stages of their linguistic development. Children write best when they receive assistance and feedback as they work. They will not be turned off if their topics are self-initiated and if they can see their efforts published, displayed and read to a wider audience.

MH: Are children entering kindergarten ready to write?

PJ: In our generation, children are bombarded by environmental print and symbolism. They learn during their pre-school development to recognize, interpret and reproduce what they see. Through scribbling (the earliest stages of a child's writing development), youngsters claim writing and the use of writing tools as fundamentals of their literacy heritage. The school must nurture, sustain and develop these initial ventures. Before they enter kindergarten, children have watched their parents write. Many have experienced writing at home during their play. They come to school expecting to write. Kindergarten teachers should be prepared to provide fat magic markers, paper and encouragement. Children are ready to "sign in" by writing their names and relevant information about self and family. They must be permitted to name, label, draw and scribble in integrated art and language exercises. The right classroom climate and a knowledgeable and caring teacher are the first priorities for a writing-led curriculum beginning at the kindergarten level.

Public Education

(*The Appeel*, March 1987)

Peter Jailall (McBride Avenue P.S.) discusses his thoughts on public education with Mike Harmer (Clifton P.S.)

MH: What exactly is your vision of the virtues and responsibilities of public education?

PJ: At the centre of public education resides the democratic distribution of rationality. By rationality I mean dispositions, beliefs and rights. In public schools we view students as rational beings and so we attempt to provide experiences and resources that enable children to construct reasonable beliefs based on sound evidence. Teaching in public schools is an act of reason, the practice of open-ended inquiry and open-minded thought.

MH: Is it fair to say that you invest the word "public" with a special significance, given the integral role of education and the pluralism of Canadian society?

PJ: Public schools, as an appendage of the state, are organized in such a way as to accept all children regardless of race and creed in our multicultural and multireligious society. In public schools we promote equality of educational opportunity for all students without reference to cultural derivation or social circumstance. As partners with the state, we help to advance certain benefits that have "spill over" effects in Canadian society at large. We seek to keep young people from harm, the harm that ignorance, political naïveté and economic incompetence can produce. I think it's important that public education stress a secular curriculum— religion can be studied as a human component, a sociological phenomenon perhaps, but worship and doctrine belong elsewhere.

MH: What's the role of public education in terms of a child's development and sense of self?

PJ: Public schools are the first social institutions that many of our young people come in contact with. It is essential that we continue to cherish and preserve our students' positive self-concept. They must be made to feel like equal participants and significant contributors. They must be helped to appreciate the importance of freedom of thought, belief and expression, and to pursue their interests, develop their talents, tackle their weaknesses and overcome their insecurities.

MH: *In the "big picture," what kind of graduates should we be striving to produce?*

PJ: Good students. Young people able to think creatively and independently, exercise self-sufficiency, respect our democratic way of life and religious and cultural co-existence, be responsible for their own behaviour and sensitive to the needs and plights of others.

Children at Kamwata School in Moruca

Discipline

(*The Appeel*, December 1986)

Another session with Peter Jailall (McBride Avenue P.S.) and Mike Harmer Clifton P.S.)

MH: I know you're itching to right some wrongs with respect to the way we, as a system, maintain discipline in our schools.

PJ: I think we tend to see discipline only as the responsibility of school administrators, the top-down imposition of remote rules and regulations and dire consequences by an arbitrary supremo. I see it as a communal exercise—the child, the school, the home. Our ultimate concern should be the growth of student self-discipline, not the punishment of "young offenders."

MH: I don't think you'll get many arguments about the need to nurture self-discipline and a sense of responsibility. I'd like to think that every school stresses positive reinforcement and reasonable expectations in its discipline procedures. But I'm not sure we should be ceding too much decision-making authority to the youngsters—you surely can't mean that student bodies should be self-regulating?

PJ: The very young need direction and guidance of course. But there has to be an incremental provision of more latitude, more responsibility, a louder voice, as students mature. We are witnessing a struggle for equal status among groups in society— women, blacks, seniors, the handicapped—and young people from one of those groups. The students' struggle to secure equal rights in decision-making is curbed and suppressed. We are afraid to give them more responsibility because we don't trust them to use it wisely. No wonder so many of them drop out of school as soon as they are able. Research done in Toronto shows a greater than 30% dropout rate of students in secondary school. Poor self-esteem coupled with the "iron fist" mentality of their overseers are largely to blame. I've no time for the school of thought that says we have to "sit on them for their own good." Too much valuable instructional time is spent on mindless discipline.

MH: I hear what you're saying and I'm sure that some of us resort to the stern lecture and the acid tongue when a positive stroke and a sympathetic ear would be more appropriate, but I think that our indictment is too general. I believe that *good educators seek to make a learning experience out of every ill-conceived or reckless or malicious behaviour. It's fertile ground for object lessons in values, respect for others, socialization skills, safety, anticipation of consequences, etc. Having said that, I also think that there has to be a certain nuclear set of rules and routines that are commonly accepted and immutable, rules which, if contravened, invoke appropriate but non-negotiable consequences.*

PJ: I take your point when it involves threats to human dignity or public safety. But it's the kinds of consequences that we choose that rankle. We use schoolwork as a punitive measure (writing lines, doing extra math questions), or we issue detentions, or we stand them in the corner, or we belittle them with sarcasm, or we ostracize them inside the school or send them home altogether. This is corrective discipline that seldom corrects. We are turning them off school. What has it all to do with our avowed intention to humanize, to build self-concept, to foster personal growth, to teach the "whole child?" The young are misunderstood. We don't spend enough time listening to their anxieties and aspirations. We don't spend enough time investigating the true causes of their hostility and mischief and malfeasance. We don't often appreciate the rigours of family dynamics and peer pressure, societal demands and cultural differences, physiological changes and doubts and fears and emotions and temptations.

MH: The counsel of the "wise and judicious parent" by all means but some children will defy your every effort to be reasonable and solicitous. When it comes to the dyed-in-the-wool incorrigibles, arbitrary measures may be all that's left, i.e. when the viability of the classroom program and/or the rights and interests of the student populace are at stake.

PJ: Praise and reward and intellectual challenge in the classroom are the answer. Regimental sergeant-majors, Etonian house masters, inquisition, martial law—none of it has any place in a modern, enlightened school system.

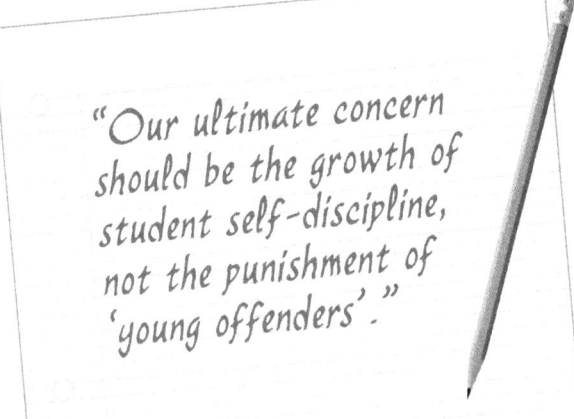

"Our ultimate concern should be the growth of student self-discipline, not the punishment of 'young offenders'."

Literacy in Our Schools

(*The Appeal*, November 1986)

Peter Jailall (McBride Ave. PS) and Mike Harmer (Clifton PS) are at it again:

MH: Heavy title! What meaning do you bring to the word "literacy?"

PJ: I see it as the life blood of our western civilization. It is part of our social and cultural heritage and it functions as a preservative of our democratic institutions. Our civilization is not restricted to an oral tradition, but to a written one as well. Part of our responsibility as literate persons is to pass down our literary heritage—writing, reading, art, music—to future generations. This momentous transfer is carried out daily throughout our society in general and our schools in particular. In school, literacy is used as a powerful tool to facilitate the cognitive skills necessary in the development of our technological, scientific and political activities.

MH: We feel the earth tremors of those dire statistics—one million illiterate adults in Canada, five million adults at a pre-secondary school reading level. I just pray we don't frighten ourselves into lowering our ambitions for education. Surely basic functional literacy is a start, not an end. I want students to experience the power and subtlety of language, the joy of fine literature, the exhilaration of debate, the challenge of creative problem-solving, and divergent thinking—what "Suzuki" calls the "precious dimension of being human." How do we do it?

PJ: Researchers like Wells, Tizzard and Clay have shown that the home is the foundation stone for literacy development in young children. They further show that students come to school ready to acquire more literacy information from the school environment. It is important for educators to sustain children's curiosity and desire in their literacy development. How can we narrow the gap between "home language" and "school language?" Is our school's philosophy relevant to the ways in which children acquire literacy skills? To promote literacy our schools should be places that foster a climate for literacy development—learning places that are non-threatening and inviting to teachers and learners alike. Environments that are humane are seedbeds for literacy development.

    The curriculum should be easily negotiated between teachers and learners to encourage proficient language use across the classroom program. The idea of conferring should be extended from the writing process to all areas of the curriculum. This can encourage students to reflect on what they are doing and promote critical thinking.

Writing should continue to have a prominent place in all areas of the program. We should continue to encourage children to write about their own ideas and, at the same time teach them how to acquire information from books. Language activities should be more than spelling drills and comprehension skills. We should be making full use of drama and puppetry. We should be allowing children to explore and model on the classical literature of the old masters and the visual literature of film.

MH: Social interaction is all important. Children must be encouraged to speak and listen, observe and speculate, experiment and take risks. Responding to people and circumstances helps them to structure their own sense of their environment. We must be there to provide the spur and the scaffolding and the sounding board. We have to recognize the sovereignty of their original thoughts while introducing new concepts and challenges. And we have to share. Our students have to see us as readers and writers. The conference has to take the place of the red pencil.

I think I'm inclined to be more cautious than you in the use of books and films as models for young creators. Basic language acquisition, of course, grammar mechanics, certainly, form and voice and character development, I suppose; but so often originality gets strangled by style that is blatantly imitative and content that is sadly derivative.

PJ: Granted, but discretion and judicious use are the keys. We can also look at human resources as models—visiting authors, artists in the schools, teaming youngsters with older students, slow learners with bright children, ESL/D students with proficient language users—peer mentors. By doing so, we will be making learning a co-operative task rather than a competitive, insular exercise.

> "Part of our responsibility as literate persons is to pass down our literary heritage – writing, reading, art, music – to future generations."

Syntax Error

(*The Appeel*, February 1987)

Peter Jailall (McBride Ave. PS) and Mike Harmer (Clifton PS) continue their give and take:

PJ: I have some concerns about the use of computers at the primary level, especially as it relates to the writing process. When children use writing tools—pencil, magic marker, crayon—they are in control. The tools are small and manageable, easily encompassed and manipulated. They can muse and tap and chew on the ends and doodle as they contemplate ideas. These instruments of writing are very close to the "self." On the other hand, children do not have direct control over the computer as an instrument of writing. Its operation is outside of the "self."

MH: I'm with you up to a point. It's a bit like the question of the two-handed writer (word processor) versus the one-handed writer (pen). I know I'm a one-handed writer. I need to feel and see the words swoop across the page, to scratch out and underline and caret and alter. I'm not sure that means that everyone needs that kind of physical/tactile reinforcement. It's a different kind of manipulation, to be sure, but I fancy the computer literate, video vet youngsters feel every bit as comfortable and in control at the keyboard as they do pen in hand.

PJ: Young children's typing on the computer is a repetitive, production line activity repeating one physical activity. Writing on paper involves the physical organization and arrangement of space.

Then too, children's writing thrives on and takes its character from prosodic marks—they'll add colour, trace over and over to show emphasis, underline three times, embroider with hand-tooled graphics, etc.—which express the author's feelings. There is no way, at the moment, for the computer to simulate that kind of exercise.

MH: I'll have to give you that one. I must admit there's something rather anonymous and other-worldly about letters magically appearing on a screen and ribbons of paper curling out of a printer. But personally, I think you made up the word "prosodic."

PJ: Don't be prosaic! Continuing in the same vein, I think it's important that children experience all the stages of writing development from pictorial representation to unidentifiable scribble to halting print to intelligible cursive hand. The computer may impede that process. Children's handwriting is also a cherished bastion of personal identity and style. Print on a monitor is physically remote and impersonal. The loops and curves and individual character of the written word become cold and uniform and linear on the screen.

MH: *One could argue that primary print and penmanship lessons seek to impose the same kind of uniformity—ball and stick, touch the line, finger space between letters, slant to the right. I think your fears about some kind of calligraphic short circuit or atrophy are unfounded. Surely no one is suggesting that the C64 is going to supplant the trusty HB! Writing will always be a skill to be mastered, like brushing teeth, spooning food and colouring inside the lines.*

PJ: I suppose I'm more cynical in that respect. I can see a time coming when children will become so reliant on the limited physical routine of pecking at the keys that small muscle development and fine motor skills will suffer.

MH: *The other side of that coin is the facility and expedience the computer provides for those who struggle with writing because the physical task of producing words on paper is a constant trial. For some the joy of imaginative thought and descriptive language is squelched by the demands of acceptable surface structure.*

PJ: How about the general effect that the presence of a computer has on the primary classroom? I'm afraid I see it as a fundamentally anti-social device. At a recent conference Bob Barton stressed the importance of the involvement of the whole group in talk and mime and song and play. The computer can only accommodate one or two students at a time. It's an essentially lonely experience. Soliloquy takes the place of dialogue. The vital personal contact of teacher and classmates is removed from the equation.

MH: *Surely a skilful teacher in a warm, supportive classroom atmosphere need have no fears on that count. The computer will be recognized for what it is—an advance in instructional technology, one more way of enhancing and diversifying program delivery. All of its audio-visual forerunners have evoked the same kind of groundless apprehension, I'm sure; the dynamic human element is still what education is all about.*

Multicultural Education

(*The Appeal*, March 1986)

This is the third instalment of the continuing conversation between Mike Harmer (MH) and Peel educator/author Peter Jailall (PJ):

MH: What demographic considerations make multicultural education so vital in Peel?

PJ: Over 100 different nationalities, speaking more than 50 different languages, have replaced the Mississauga Indians who once farmed in sprawling communities across the region. The 1981 Census figures reveal that Peel is more ethnic than the whole province put together. 43.8% of Peel's population is listed as belonging to origins other than English or French. Pearson International Airport is a gateway for new immigrants entering our region. At the same time, there continues to be spiral growth in new family housing. Peel is one of the fastest-growing multicultural centres in the country. Our school population is increasingly enhanced by children from all manner of cultural, linguistic, racial and religious backgrounds.

MH: What does multicultural education mean?

PJ: The essence of what it means to be a Canadian lies in our cultural diversity. Multicultural education means teaching children to understand and respect different cultures so that they can be prepared for living in our multicultural community. The preparation for life in Canadian society should be encouraged in schools by developing programs that emphasize equality of opportunity, a sense of belonging, a sense of being treated fairly, and a feeling of high self-esteem. A democratic society is judged by the way its minorities are treated.

MH: Is it fair, then to think of multicultural education as the teaching of "survival skills" for life in a multicultural society, the global village, etc.?

PJ: All of us have roots and as Canadians, many of us hold dual loyalties. We are, at the same time, members of an ethnic group and individual Canadian citizens. Our identity is the "salad bowl" concept of nationhood, as opposed to our steaming "melting pot" neighbour to the south. We need to educate students to appreciate their own cultures so that they are able to acknowledge and appreciate the cultures of others.

MH: Jack Kehoe urges that we not solve problems that aren't there. But how are we to deal with the problems that are there in the classroom—name-calling, language difficulties, entrenched learning styles, exclusionary cultural or religious beliefs?

PJ: As teachers we cannot be held accountable for all of society's problems. But, in the context of our classrooms, we can be instrumental in changing negative attitudes that hurt others. It is our duty to condemn bigotry in the school environment and to teach respect and tolerance. To remain silent is to condone name-calling. A child whose full "citizenship" in the classroom community is not validated enthusiastically by the teacher is a child with a poor self-concept, low academic achievement, and even deviant behaviour. Teachers must respect the language that children bring from home. The language that newcomers already possess can be used to teach the language they need. We work for a public school board and serve a community and as teachers we should respect the religious rights and ethnic identities of all children.

MH: How must teachers be prepared to change?

PJ: One of the challenges facing education today is teacher change. Some teachers become defensive and dig in their heels when the need for change is mentioned. Most of us are comfortable with the familiar and threatened by the unfamiliar. Most teachers were trained to deal with a school population that was, by and large, culturally homogeneous. Today the cultures many children bring to school seem to be at variance with the cultural values held by the teachers themselves. A program of in-service training may well be needed to help teachers understand the youngsters of the nineties and the myriad diversities inherent in a truly multicultural society.

> "Multicultural education means teaching children to understand and respect different cultures so that they can be prepared for living in our multicultural community."

Women in Education

(*The Appeal*, April 1986)

Mike Harmer (MH) and Peter Jailall (PJ) tackle another topical subject this month:

MH: Is it too facile to suggest that it's because of their natural maternalism that there is a preponderance of women in the primary division?

PJ: Both in the home and at school, women have always been actively involved in the ethic of care, and they are fully experienced and qualified to train primary children. Centuries of mothering make them good at working with young children. It's long overdue that their efforts in this sometimes tedious, but more often joyous, endeavour were properly acknowledged. Women are not biologically predisposed to teach at the primary level. Men can also be socialized and trained to teach the very young. Many are gravitating to the primary grades with success.

MH: Do you see the two genders bringing fundamentally different traits, strengths, interests and sensitivities to the classroom?

PJ: Primary children are not significantly influenced by the gender of the teacher if that person is truly professional, knowledgeable, sensitive to individual needs and happy in his/her work. With older children, the picture changes somewhat. Adolescent girls may well need a strong female role model, i.e. one that combines a career orientation with home and family responsibilities. Adolescent boys may also find it easier to confide in a male teacher. Men and women working side by side are perhaps the optimal situation. Children from single parent homes may find it beneficial to associate with a teacher surrogate for the missing parent.

MH: Have women received their due recognition in education?

PJ: I think not. Perhaps because women have been traditionally identified with roles that have been arbitrarily relegated, in the perception of many, to lesser importance (secretaries, lunch "ladies," nurses, parent volunteers, teacher aides), full credit for their contributions to education has been slow to surface. In 1936 Maclean's published an article entitled "Is the School Marm a Menace?" This article, written by a male principal, described "the weakest feature in the system" as "the woman teacher." Women have woven an admirable, if virtually invisible, history of service to education. How many schools are named after them?

MH: The management, the administration, the direction of education is still male-dominated. How can women shift the balance?

PJ: There are signs that Peel's "perpetual patriarchy" in the realm of school and system management is wavering. Capable, intelligent women continue to serve in silent, subordinate roles, but more and more are being encouraged to test the administrative waters. It's a long road. Women (and members of visible minorities) must be steadfast in their aspirations and assiduous in their preparations. One hopes and anticipates that the new Equal Opportunity Policy will help ensure that positions of responsibility are open to all candidates with legitimate claims.

MH: What are your views on the provincial amalgamation of the affiliates of OTF?

PJ: I think that, as a professional body, we need to speak with one voice and work with one agenda. As teachers we must set an example to society in general, and to our students in particular. We must demonstrate that men and women, elementary and secondary teachers, public and separate teachers, can work together as members of one professional body.

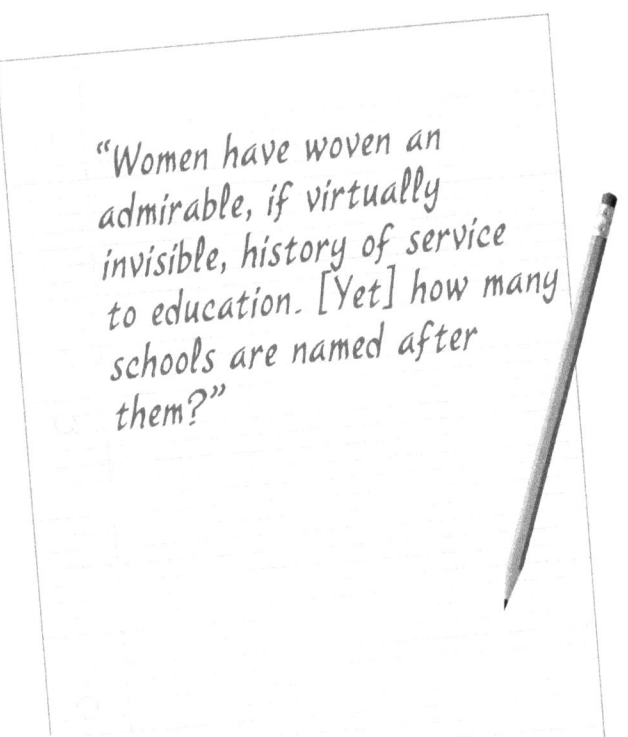

"Women have woven an admirable, if virtually invisible, history of service to education. [Yet] how many schools are named after them?"

Monologues

Concerning Education

Teaching at the edge of the rainforest

Message from Ernie Kuechmeister

If words and ideas are the seeds and plants, and writing the soil, then the teacher is the gardener and children's stories are the fruit. And so the analogy carries us into the growth cycles of change and yields the memories that, in turn, provide the landscape of our lives.

Peter Jailall, colleague and friend, is a master gardener in the veritable "Children's Garden of Verses." In this collection of writing that spans over 30 years of service in the schools of the Region of Peel, he has managed to give us a glimpse into the process where both teachers and students grow together in their understanding of themselves, their communities, their world.

Enjoy the journey and be inspired to begin your own logbook or diary. Or better still, share the experience with a child.

Ernie Kuechmeister
Principal (retired Peel District School Board)

Children playing at recess at Wallaba School

Radwanski Reviewed

By Peter Jailall, McBride Avenue P.S.
(*The Beacon*, March 1998)

Many of us will welcome the March break if only to recover from a series of recent attacks on the school system and on the work we do with students in schools.

First, there is the Radwanski Report. The report calls for a return to the basics because schools are not giving students the skills necessary to function in the workplace. It recommends province-wide standardized testing at "appropriate levels."

Mention is also made of the bureaucratic structure of high schools and the high dropout rate among secondary students.

Then, there is our federal Minister of Sports and Culture lashing out against the school system. In his summary at the end of the Winter Olympic Games in Calgary he said, "Physical education in our schools is a disgrace to Canada."

This is an unfair criticism on the Minister's part. Our schools are not operated solely by the state. In our democracy, we happen to have different bodies that exercise their group rights, as well as their individual rights, where the education of their children is concerned. The teaching of physical education may not be their top priority. Also, school boards need heavy financing to help defray liability costs. Is the Minister prepared to pay liability insurance for school boards? And finally, we cannot afford to give extra time and attention to physical education (important as it may be) when we are dealing with an overcrowded curriculum.

There still exists among us a few "diehards" who keep insisting on "basics" and "skills" only, as if teachers have abandoned teaching the basic skills in the academic curriculum. It is not only our responsibility to teach "basics" and "skills." People in business and industry also have a responsibility to train their employees in the necessary skills relevant to the conditions in their own workplace. Are they making a full contribution to this social responsibility?

Standardized testing is a very inadequate yardstick to measure a student's ability. We can train students in schools to pass tests and we can gear our teaching to meet the requirements of those tests. But are we engaged in educating young people in the fullest sense of the word?

Here in Ontario, we have been doing an excellent job educating our young people. The business community in particular has gained tremendously from our efforts. We have an education system here that is comparable to any other in the world.

We have been preparing generations of Ontarians to live and work in a democratic tradition. By precept and by example we have been conveying to our students what it really means to be a good Canadian citizen and a member of a community. "Basics" and "skills" for us mean more than sums and sentence structure.

They mean teaching our young people the skills of living and working co-operatively and with distinct group values. We try to help our students develop meaning in their lives as they grow as individuals, respecting the point of view of others. We have also been preparing our students to ask intelligent questions and to make sensible decisions. In short, we try to give them the tools necessary to keep on learning in the university of life. Learning for us does not end in schools.

We have been saddled with the added responsibility of helping other institutions—civic and cultural, the home, the church and the business community. We are not miracle workers. We do need the full financial and moral support of governments, and all the other institutions, to continue creating a vibrant society.

Here in Peel we have been doing our part in giving high school students real life skills in the workplace. But we need to do more. We can help to prevent students from dropping out of high school by inviting them to negotiate the curriculum with us and by making schoolwork relevant to their cultural and interest needs. And do they have to attend school at the higher grades if they don't want to? Apprenticeship training in the workplace may be the answer.

> "We can help to prevent students from dropping out of high school by inviting them to negotiate the curriculum with us and by making schoolwork relevant to their cultural and interest needs."

Teacher Bashing

By Peter Jailall, Queenston Drive P.S.

Teacher bashers have always been and will always be with us, but we are now witnessing a sharp escalation in teacher bashing, especially during this period of economic hardship. And we are getting tired of it. We are getting tired of being blamed for all of today's ills in society—violence in schools, misbehaving children, absentee parents, changing family structures, massive unemployment and increased taxation.

Take counsellor Evelyn Dodds' comments for example. This Thunder Bay politician is calling on taxpayers to wage a war on teachers. She said, "I think the education system will be improved only when it's completely destroyed and rebuilt." (Toronto Star, March, 1992)

She called our federations "powerful, vicious monsters." This woman wants blood. She is playing on the fears of taxpayers. She is expressing a biased, simplistic view as she deals with such a complex issue as education.

She fails to see any good coming out of the schools and so she wants to shut them down. Her irresponsible call for the destruction of our education system smacks of teacher bashing of the most vicious kind. Critics like her, who are not directly involved in teaching children, make this false assumption that anyone who has been in school is an expert. They can speak with authority about teachers and teaching. She should spend a month in an elementary classroom to find out what it's really like. As a professional body we do not poke our noses in the offices of other professions, making sweeping generalizations about areas of work we do not understand. It's time we stand up to our critics. For too long we have been apologetic and quiet about our role in society.

We mould minds of this nation and we are proud of it. A nation's political leaders ought to be proud of its teachers too. And we would like to remind Counsellor Dodds that she once sat in our classrooms.

Teachers in the elementary grades continue to struggle daily against adverse conditions and misinformed critics to give our children a good education. We are not only teachers for money and holidays. Teaching for the vast majority of us is a vocation not just a job.

The Education System, Counsellor Dodds, cannot be destroyed. Like society itself, it changes slowly. And in regards to our monster unions, you better stay out of their way because they will gobble you up.

"No Minister!"

By Peter Jailall, Munden Park P.S.
(*The Beacon*, February 1996)

Onta-ri-a-ri-a-ri-o —no more a place for our children to stand, and no more a place for them to grow—not even the place we used to know.

We are living in mean times, with mean-spirited leaders talking nonsense instead of formulating sound educational policies. As a result, both our children's future and the future of our profession hang in the balance.

Teachers are disappointed, worried and angry about the government's rumoured cutbacks in education.

The politicians want our planning time—time we fought so hard for in the past, time that helps maximize learning for the children we teach. The rhythm of the school is so fast that teachers are always busy teaching, preparing lessons or supervising children. We use planning time to talk about ways of helping children improve their learning, to make important phone calls to parents, and to engage in the dialogue that is so necessary for our professional growth.

For the past three years, Peel teachers have exercised a lot of patience and understanding. We have had no increase in salary and we have lost many of our colleagues. We continue to live under the burden of "Rae Days." We do not, as our critics would have us believe, "have it so good!"

Some teachers are angry with a perceived lack of leadership at the top. In times like these, we need leaders to instil confidence and assurance… not to predict doom and gloom. Never before in the history of our profession has there been so much fear, uncertainty and low teacher morale. We are afraid of job loss, of poor working conditions, and, most of all, of all of the detrimental effects these cutbacks will have on our children in years to come.

This year the government will be cutting $400 million. How much will they cut next year? Already we are seeing signs of the trouble ahead. The parents of many of the children we teach are unemployed. Single mothers continue to bring up children on their own, while teachers work even harder to help these children adjust socially and emotionally in the classroom. Many children cannot afford to pay for school trips. Some come to school hungry, while others are in need of winter clothing. Some children, who internalize the dreadful economic conditions at home, carry heavy adult burdens to school. Teachers intervene to meet the mental health needs of these children all the time. Our job is not to drill facts, but to teach the whole child.

Daily we face new challenges emanating from the changing patterns of family life, changes in the workplace—the pain of a sluggish economy. In spite of all these external forces, we are called upon to model moral behaviour, buoyant optimism, a sense of humour, a caring concern for all our students, and the "joys of lifelong learning." Our children are truly fortunate to have skilled, knowledgeable, conscientious and mentally healthy teachers. What more can the ministry or the board ask of teachers?

We ask that the government make the cuts less drastic—for the children's sake. We also ask that the politicians listen to the voices of the teachers on the front line. We need more dialogue, more consultation. We must resist cuts that impede our work with children.

On December 13, hundreds of teachers from Peel marched in front of the Minister's constituency office to protest the cuts. Again, on January 13, thousands of teachers rallied at Queen's Park to protest the cuts. We must be prepared to keep on delivering the message. Parents must join us to protect their children's future. If we do not stand up now, collectively, to protest the cutbacks in education, they'll take away our planning time, eliminate our PA days, cut our salaries, lay off more teachers, and give us larger classes to teach. If this happens, surely the children of Ontario, our future, will be harmed. Put down the axe, Mr. S!

Peter with teacher at Wallaba School

Creating A Crisis

By Peter Jailall, Munden Park P.S.
(*The Beacon*, November 1997)

Ever since he took on the education portfolio two years ago, John Snobelen has been on the warpath against teachers. At the outset he said he would create a crisis.

And he did.

He has consistently picked holes in the education system, devalued the teaching profession and has lashed out against the dignity of teachers. Early in his reign, he announced that the system was broken and boasted about his toolkit to fix it.

He saw no need to engage in any kind of meaningful dialogue with teachers, their federations or the school boards. Instead, he set himself up as a knight in shining armour, the hero bent on cleaning up the education system. He criticized teachers' work and called for more testing and competition with other provinces. He talked glibly about schooling—the filling of children's heads with facts and figures, demanding more time from the school day to do that.

He never talked about educating the whole child and teaching children how to learn and of teaching for good citizenship. His agenda was obviously not about the education of Ontario's children, but "Creating a Crisis" to suit his government's calculated political agenda. When the Harris government came to power, it promised to reduce taxes by 30%. Already, they have taken $600 million out of the education budget. Now they want to bleed the system of yet another billion dollars. And Bill 160 empowers them to do just that.

Instead of "fixing the system," they are dismantling it. Big Brothers Harris, Snobelen and Johnson profess to know exactly what's best for everyone in Ontario—students, parents and teachers. Bill 160 would give them control over taxing municipalities and spending in areas they think are important or necessary. In the Tories' move to centralize education, Ontarians can expect the disappearance of local school communities. Local autonomy will be gone and decisions on the operation of the province's schools would come from Queen's Park, not from local residents.

Absolute power would reside in the hands of Mr. Johnson, an official not accountable to collective agreement between teachers and school boards. The minister of Education would be in a position to use Bill 160 to set teachers' working conditions, class sizes and planning time. He would have the power to bring in non-certified teachers into Ontario schools, a situation sure to cause conflict among existing staff. These non-certified teachers would not be under the jurisdiction of the Ontario College of Teachers, an institution Mr. Snobelen himself helped to create.

Mr. Johnson, his boss Mike Harris and members of the Education Improvement Commission, including Dave Cooke, Minister of Education in the previous NDP government, have no time for teachers' unions or school boards. They are bent on using this absolute power to control Ontario's Education System. And this is what teachers and most parents are opposing.

I have attended rallies and demonstrations in Peel, at Maple Leaf Gardens and at Queen's Park. I have never seen so many teachers and parents so angry, so united and so determined to fight for the future of Ontario's children. The call to shut down the schools in the province is real. "We will not back down!" teachers say. Meanwhile, Mr. Snobelen has lost the confidence of his Premier. He refused to listen to the united voices of teachers. He dismissed the views of students, many of whom are very informed about the issues.

Many parents were also concerned about Mr. Snobelen's political game playing. They know his number. Our new Minister, Mr. Dave Johnson, needs to know that there can be no education system without qualified, well-prepared, dedicated teachers.

He needs to be told that the job of teaching the province's youths belongs to expert educators, not ill-informed legislators.

Mr. Johnson is apparently a capable man with a reputation of consensus building. Teachers knew what they didn't like about Mr. Snobelen and Bill 160. Now we need to tell Mr. Johnson about our vision of education in the 21st century, about democracy, about public education and about education for a diverse, multicultural society.

Perhaps, this whole episode should remind us all (administrators and teachers) that we need to be more proactive as a profession.

And we must stand together as a united force.

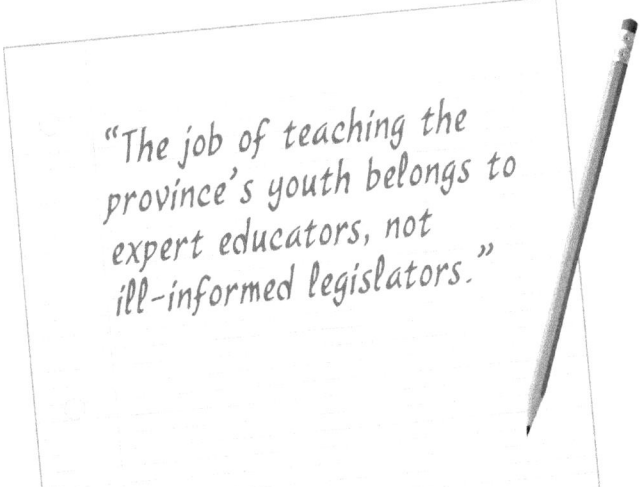

"The job of teaching the province's youth belongs to expert educators, not ill-informed legislators."

Troubled Times

By Peter Jailall, Munden Park P.S.
(*The Beacon*, June 1996)

It is true that we are living in mean economic times, when all levels of government, corporations and boards of education are called upon to make sacrifices. But, even in terrible times like these, the education of young Canadians needs the support of all of our institutions, public and private. We cannot take the future generation for granted. Money and time invested in the young now will pay dividends later, and all of society will be the beneficiary. It's a case of being penny wise and pound foolish. As teachers, we know that the general public—parents, administrators, politicians—has high expectations of us. We also know that our role is vital to the well-being of our democratic society. But we do get impatient, even angry, when "experts" make statements and pass judgement as if they know what goes on in classrooms. Our composure is truly tested when silly, simplistic statements are made in high places.

Since the beginning of this school year, schools and school people have been the targets of attacks. Politicians have been talking about schooling and training…but not about education. For the record, some clarification is necessary:

Schooling vs Education

What has been talked about in the media and the legislature is schooling. The debate on schooling is associated with vocational development, with the teaching of skills and drills, and with the cramming of facts.

In schools, professional teachers have been involved with the education of children. We know that education is a lifelong process which has to do with social, emotional, moral and ethical values. We talk about learning that provides an understanding of science, technology and care of our environment. Education in Peel classrooms includes an appreciation of beauty and excellence, as well as an understanding of human relationships. Our brand of education also includes what it means to be a citizen in today's multicultural, multiracial Ontario.

We teach young people daily to develop social skills, to work and get along with others, to understand group values, and to respect the positions and points of view expressed by others. We work hard to help develop the individual's sense of self-worth and emotional well-being. We cherish and praise hard work, but we also expose our students to leisure activities. Yes, we prepare them for "the good life" in a democracy that is still strong and free.

So, when our detractors and legislation shapers talk only about "schooling" and not about "education" in the fullest sense of the word, they are confusing the issues and the public. Our task as teachers is far more complex and important than flipping burgers and filling potholes.

School Councils

Teachers and administrators in a school have rarely worked alone. There is usually some form of school council, however casual and informal, around them. With the decline of the church and other social and cultural organizations, the school remains the hub of community activities. We continue to work with doctors, nurses, psychologists, police officers and other child care workers. Make no mistake, we are the most visible and accessible institution in our communities today.

We must be careful, however, to ensure that school councils understand their advisory mandate, that their agendas and vested interests are not allowed to deviate from the enhancement of student learning and social interaction. School councils vary from community to community, depending on the culture of each school, its diversity and student needs.

What Most Teachers Want

- the good staff morale necessary to improve the quality of instruction for children
- the full support of the administration in the monumental task of teaching children
- a strong and united Educators' Association focusing on the efforts of the constituent federations to the benefit of all children
- more staff collaboration to lighten the load for each teacher and maximize learning for children
- whatever is necessary to save the careers of the youngest members of our profession

Future Trends/Unanswered Questions

1. Will the Ministry take over school boards, making of the GTA one huge educational zone?
2. Can the "corporate agenda" be part of the education system?
3. To what extent should school services be made available to pre-school children?
4. Should public schooling be 100% publicly funded?
5. Is the Peel Board of Education too big to manage?
6. How can equality of educational opportunity be assured for all students?

"...we better pray"

By Peter Jailall, Munden Park P.S.
(The Beacon, December 1996)

"A horrible thing is coming this way

> Creeping closer day by day Its eyes are scary
> It growls, it groans…
> It spreads its wings
> It belches flame
> It has no name
> I tell you Judge, we better pray."

This poem, an untrue tale by Harvey Zemach, describes the true feelings of Ontario's teachers in general, and Peel's teachers in particular, especially when we consider the step-by-step, torturous, unpredictable announcements and pronouncements regarding educational policies and funding cuts. We continue to be troubled, both about the status of our profession and the future of Ontario's children.

Daily, we await the next announcements, sometimes in fear, sometimes in anger. We continue to await the decision of the Who Does What panel on the fate of the Greater Toronto Area, as well as news of the possible abolition of school boards. Many of us hope that this will never happen. If it does, we will see the destruction of Peel's unique communities, held together by our schools through the years.

On November 23, the Minister, the Hon. John Snobelen, made yet another major announcement. This time he called for a "vigorous and demanding curriculum"—a curriculum for grades one to nine focusing on reading, writing, spelling, grammar, mathematics, science, geography and Canadian history. He further called on parents and the public to "grade" our efforts. The Minister outlined in detail what we will be expected to teach in each grade. "We have to do more with less," he warned.

Again, the Minister is making false assumptions about teaching and learning. For those teachers who would like to see spelling, grammar, reading and writing integrated across the curriculum, his directives will pose some confusion and problems. It seems he would have us teach the different components of the language arts program as separate entities or disciplines. His "structured" and "direct" approach to teaching and learning is not consistent with current research about how children learn.

We know as teachers that children have different styles of learning and different cognitive abilities. We know that they learn at different rates. Are we expected to fail those children in the primary grades who have not attained an arbitrary goal or level? There is, in every classroom, a wide spectrum of abilities, interests, expressive preferences, task commitments, personalities, etc. How will the Minister's vision of "standardization" accommodate this diversity? Where do learning disabled students fit in the Minister's scheme of things? Peel is home to many recent immigrant children whose first language is neither English nor French. How can a prescriptive, "standardization" curriculum meet the needs of these E.S.L./E.S.D. learners? The Minister seems to focus on basics only, the task of putting children through their academic paces. Such "training" would not seem to acknowledge the education of the whole child. Play, a significant way to learn in the primary grades, would appear to have no place in Mr. Snobelen's no-nonsense curriculum.

In Peel, we have to carry a load even heavier than the Minister has ordered. We already teach all the "basics" he has outlined.

We assess constantly in different, meaningful ways, and we educate children who come from diverse cultural and linguistic backgrounds. We deal constantly with social problems that show up in our classrooms, problems that those in power often ignore or pretend don't exist. We educate the whole child.

Today's classroom is unlike the classroom of the fifties that many of our critics attended. The place called "school" has changed. Today's classroom in unlike the orderly, monocultural setting of yesteryear. Its rhythm and dynamics are least understood by those who work elsewhere and rarely, if ever, set foot in a school. It's not easy to appreciate what goes on in the modern classroom unless you live in a modern classroom on a daily basis.

And so we wait for the next lump of coal in our educational stocking… Merry Christmas!

> "It's not easy to appreciate what goes on in the modern classroom unless you live in a modern classroom on a daily basis."

Talking Back

By Peter Jailall, Munden Park P.S.
(The Beacon)

Sometimes in the mornings, some children come to school tired from lack of sleep the night before. They have been watching television, playing Nintendo, listening to CDs or just hanging out late in the malls. As soon as the first lesson starts, some begin to yawn. You can spit out loonies while reading a story to them, yet they will not listen attentively.

Some children come to school hungry because no one is at home to help them prepare a meal, or to make sure they eat. A few survive on junk food. Children are sad because their parents have been laid off. Others who come from broken homes are angry most of the time. One girl from Bosnia cries regularly in class because she worries constantly about her father's safety over there.

Children come to school daily with heavy burdens and many depend on us to help them unload these burdens.

Children need to resolve their personal problems before they can even begin to concentrate on academic work.

Teaching and learning are slow processes of reflection and internalization of knowledge, ideas and attitudes. They do not only involve test scores. Our job is not like digging ditches—the more you dig, the further you go. It's also about educating the emotions of young people in the nineties, preparing them to cope in hard times.

So when the overnight "experts" engage in their empty rhetoric and try to tell us how to do our jobs, we must talk back. We do not have to wait on the federations, the Boards of Education and the politicians to talk for us. We are the experts. We are school people who struggle daily in our classrooms educating children. Children's stories spin in and out of our heads as we drive home. Their stories even follow us to bed at night.

We know how children learn. Some of us have been teaching children all our lives. We know how to modify the curriculum to meet the individual needs of our students. We don't need a blue print from the 'experts.' There seems to be a whole lot of educational experts out there telling us how to do our jobs.

The experts continue to hand us an overloaded curriculum each September. Each new school year they pick on yet another subject—AIDS prevention, drug abuse, the environment, science and technology plus the 'basics.'

They expect us to perform miracles. Our critics like to make comparisons with the Japanese system of education, a highly competitive system that most of them know little about. They never talk about the vulgar competition and the hidden dropout rate there.

We invite our critics to spend some time in classrooms working with children, not just looking around schools for a few minutes.

For too long we have been silent, working in isolated classrooms, shutting ourselves off from each other by those heavy walls. This isolation has done us a lot of harm, giving others an opportunity to appropriate our voices. We need to build a stronger colleagueship, talking and working together in collaborative settings, rather than working in isolation. We are far too fragmented as a professional body—gender divisions, administration, elementary panel, secondary panel.

We need to develop a shared, collective leadership. The recent Social Contract and the wave of uninformed criticism have been a signal for us. Now is the time for us to look beyond the four walls of our classrooms and step out to examine the system as a whole. We need to work harder on shared decision making with school principals, who, themselves feel isolated at times.

We must find a new way of talking and thinking among ourselves to counteract some of the misinformed, irresponsible statements made by lay people. As teachers working together, we have the capacity to change society more than any other professional group. We have organizational skills, knowledge and talent. Let's put them to use.

> "We are school people who struggle daily in our classrooms educating children. Children's stories spin in and out of our heads as we drive home. Their stories even follow us to bed at night."

E.Q.A.O.

By Peter Jailall, Munden Park P.S.
(*The Beacon*, April 1997)

"I feel that my students are being used as guinea pigs to suit the agenda of politicians," said Ms. M., a Grade 3 teacher with the Peel Board of Education. (Ms. M. prefers that I not use her real name).

Generally, there is silent resentment among teachers, administrators and parents with respect to the provincial Grade 3 testing initiative. Many parents, especially, have not been properly informed. The students, of course, have no say about whether or not they want to take the test… after all, they're just children. Classroom teachers are upset because they feel that the tests are being rammed down everyone's throat.

The Education Quality and Accountability Office (EQAO), a group of civil servants from Queen's Park associated with the Ministry of Education, is administering the test to 130,000 Grade 3 students across the province— at a cost of $7 million, we are told. The tests will be marked on April 18, by teachers who have no relationship with or knowledge of the students being tested.

Classroom teachers, particularly those in primary grades, have some serious concerns about this method of assessing their students. Based on what these primary teachers know about child development and different learning styles during the formative years, they see these tests as pedagogically unsound.

The paper and pencil task in the EQAO testing will not provide an accurate picture of the whole child. What about physical education, art and music? At this level, an assessment of these students' social and emotional growth and development has to be just as important as a look at how well they've mastered the 3 Rs. These are primary students who should not be expected to handle such a highly structured and protracted testing situation. Imagine testing 8 year olds for 3 hours on 10 consecutive school days! I fancy the EQAO will hesitate to put university students under such rigorous examination conditions. University students would rebel. This is not the way to assess primary students. A few bright students may acquit themselves capably. The vast majority will be frustrated.

Classroom teachers at this level observe their students at play. A major part of their assessment is obtained through observing the children using manipulatives. During play, teachers listen to children talk, and, in so doing, assess their oral language, vocabulary, grammar, even their social skills.

In play, children communicate freely and comfortably with one another... and the teacher is the wiser for it. This EQAO paper and pencil ordeal is formalized, lock step, and completely alien to primary children who are infinitely more familiar with the relaxed, supportive nature of their daily classroom routine.

As a teacher of some of these students, I read the tests. I am convinced that they are far too advanced for children in this age group. Grade 5 students would find them difficult... many parents would experience difficulty with them. A great many Grade 3 students across the Greater Toronto Area come from homes where English is used as a second language. Surely these tests are culturally biased where such students are concerned.

If these tests are continued in future years, Kindergarten and Grade 1 teachers will start preparing the students for what is to come. They will begin to teach to the test during these early years.

When the results are published, these tests will invoke an unhealthy situation of vulgar competition and comparison in our school system. Children at this age are accustomed to working collaboratively with their teachers and classmates, sharing ideas and asking questions. The EQAO testing will serve to isolate students and attach an artificial measure of confidence and individualism to their efforts. It has the potential to create fear and anxiety in tender minds. This new culture of competitive education will be pitting students against students, parents against parents.

As parents and teachers, we must be advocates for our primary students. Politicians have a way of suddenly changing educational policy to suit their own ideologies. How many hours have we spent on the implementation of the Common Curriculum, only to hear that its future is uncertain?

The EQAO Grade 3 testing program, as Ms. M. warns, may be another swing of the pendulum... back to the basics, back to a standardization of teaching methods, back to competition. And all the time, the cynics among us will be wondering whether this is less an attempt to assess our Grade 3 students and more the setting of a political agenda for the next election.

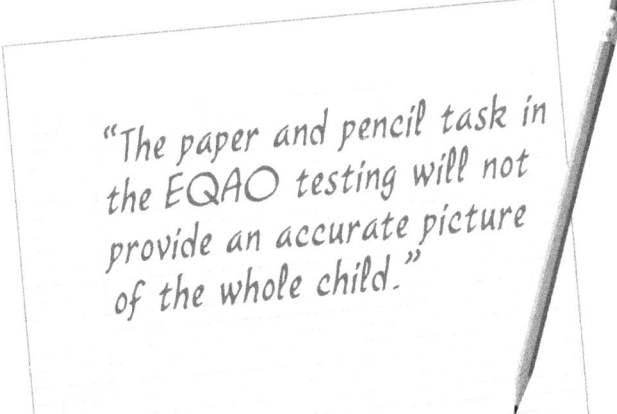

"The paper and pencil task in the EQAO testing will not provide an accurate picture of the whole child."

Children's Rights

By Peter Jailall, Queenston Drive P.S.
(October 1990)

The date—October 1st 1990; the place—New York, the city where some children sleep on the streets; the event—The Summit of the UN General Assembly meeting to talk about 40,000 children who die daily from malnutrition and disease.

Imagine, a nation of young world citizens, a capacity crowd large enough to fill the Sky Dome, dying daily. The crisis forced these world leaders to meet. But they have waited too long. This may well be just another conference where people come to talk, meet new faces and feel righteous about an issue of a universal nature, a worthwhile issue, mind you, about which no one can quarrel.

In any society, rich or poor, children are always the first to suffer when times are bad because they can least articulate their rights and because they are so economically and emotionally dependent on their adult caregivers. Adults in any part of the world have a moral responsibility to protect children from harm, to nurture their physical and emotional needs and to engage them in a full education in order to prepare them to continue in their particular pattern of culture. But adults everywhere continue to fail children.

For us teaching in Peel, this overdue UN Summit is nothing great to shout about. Generally, we care for children without tooting our horns. We read to them to make them literate, hug them to make them happy, teach them to make them confident and sometimes we even feed them to make them healthy.

Yes, there are pockets of child poverty in our country and there is child abuse, but we in the schools try not to shirk our responsibility. We in Peel have been very fortunate. I have observed children in the Developing World who are really hurting. Most of them lack the basic necessities of life—food, clothing, shelter, medical care and love. Some are growing up in war zones where bombs are falling like rain around them. Their toys consist of spent shells as they play war games practising for the real thing. They know no childhood.

For us, though, even in our comfort, the question still remains—what do we do with our pockets of poor and illiterate children? Is there a solution? At least we are making an effort to address the question of children's rights.

This sudden call for the rights of children at the UN must be seen in the general context of a western upsurge as it pertains to the rights of all categories of persons with special needs—the disabled, the elderly, single parents, new immigrants and of course, children. During the past two decades, we in the West have been placing a lot of emphasis on the rights of persons and we must continue to take the lead in this direction.

Here in Peel, if we are serious in granting children their full rights, we have to make some hard financial decisions and some heavy demands on the new provincial government as well. Educating and empowering the young is costly and sometimes we can be reluctant to spending money educating children because we do not see any immediate financial benefit. But, if we invest money sensibly on children's education, just think how much more rewarding the pay back will be for society as a whole.

If our children in Peel are to develop a strong sense of community, they need schools that are spacious, well ventilated and within their own neighbourhoods. At school, they need more creative playgrounds with suitable play materials. They deserve a curriculum that emphasizes the arts for the continued education of their emotions. They do not need to sell things in order for them to enjoy the performing arts or to own classrooms full of books. Expensive technological gadgets can wait until high school, or even until they have entered the work force where employers can then pay for training. Many children do need a hot breakfast at school, which some parents are too busy or too poor to provide. We can finance a feeding program for hungry children from funds generated by the new federal ministry responsible for children or from any of the popular fast food outlets.

Finally, our children deserve informed and caring teachers. Are we prepared to spend more on professional development?

Our task of educating children also includes standing up with them and for them at all times. At the elementary level, dedicated professionals have been very supportive, making sure that their charges are treated as persons with full rights. Even though it's our job, we remain distantly unknown to those powerful political world leaders who met recently in New York, promising to stop 40,000 kids from dying daily. We await their solution.

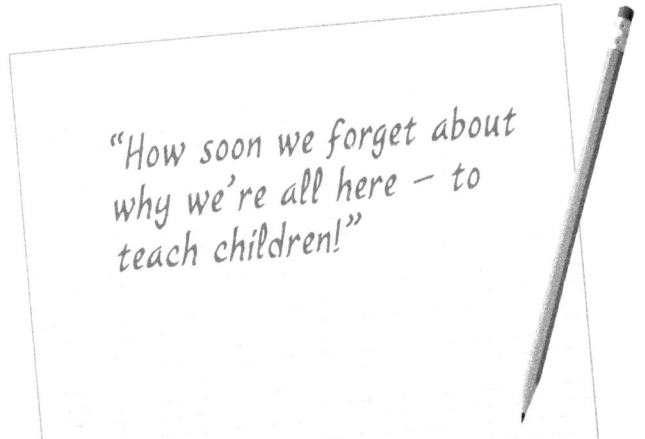

"How soon we forget about why we're all here — to teach children!"

One Profession

By Peter Jailall, McBride Avenue P.S.
(*The Appeel*, June 1987)

Another one bites the dust! Yes, it's another year under our belts. We'll leave the classroom with the satisfied tiredness born of the knowledge that we've done the job to the best of our ability. Time for a brief sigh of relief before we acknowledge that it starts all over again in September—different faces, same challenges and concerns. We reflect ruefully on our shortcomings, on things not done and expedient compromises struck. We relish the initiatives that worked and celebrate all our minor victories. But through it all shines the joy of working with young minds, of managing the shifting dynamics and reconciling the myriad differences of the classroom.

What a good job we do of encouraging students to work together, of shaping so many different dispositions and interests and attitudes and abilities into a single productive working unit! How well we preach the need for them to respect their differences and revel in their similarities. What on earth happens when it comes to embodying the same sensibilities and spirit of co-operation in our interactions with adult colleagues? We in the education community can get so intolerant and sectarian with each other, can't we?

How easily we retire into our selfish and suspicious factions: male/female, elementary/secondary, administrator/classroom teacher, French/English, public system/separate system/private system! How soon we forget about why we're all here—to teach children! It's time we recognize that we are all equal partners in the process. Our job descriptions may differ, our clientele may differ, our workplace and working conditions and remuneration may differ, but we are all educators. We must continue to talk to each other. We must begin to get rid of the false barriers, the immutable party lines, the educational jurisdictions and "team uniforms." If our ultimate aim is to educate the whole child, then we should start re-defining our role in society and our professional relationships, instead of permitting small group loyalties and self-interest to split us apart.

Labour of Love

By Peter Jailall, McBride Avenue P.S.

Teacher Sylvia Ashton-Warner, remembering a story from her experience teaching Maori and white children in a school in New Zealand, related her interaction with one of the younger members of her class.

"What is it? What is it, little one?"

I kneel to his level and tip his chin. Tears break from the big brown eyes and set off down his face.

"That's why somebodies they broke my castle for notheen. Somebodies."

I sit on my low chair in the raftered prefab, take him on my knee and tuck the black Maori head beneath my chin.

"There…there… look at my pretty boy…" But that's only a memory now. A year old.

I relived this incident, described by Sylvia Ashton-Warner in her book "Teacher," last week as I attended a memorial service for one of our colleagues, Clarence Amichand, educator and friend, from Shelter Bay Public School.

The children assembled in the gym to sing Clarence's favourite songs—"Morning Has Broken" and "Lord of the Dance." They will always remember these songs after their school life is over because music is one of the everlasting subjects we teach in the curriculum. Some of his students composed and read poems to his memory. One can see from the children's manner, behaviour and sweet singing that they were totally involved in paying full tribute to their lost teacher. It was a lesson in morality conducted by the Shelter Bay students to a big class of adults who were a very receptive audience.

Parents in the Shelter Bay community turned out in full force to pay tribute to a teacher of their children. They remembered his words of kindness, his gentle smile, and the patience he demonstrated when he taught their children to read and write. They worked hard to prepare snacks for the occasion. They were eager to show their appreciation and they did their best to make the visitors comfortable and welcome. Indeed, we are the best mediators between the Board and the community.

One lesson that we can learn from the celebration of Clarence's life is the diversity of the audience present that day. As teachers we have the capacity and the ability to bring people together, all people—the young, the old, the indifferent, and the culturally and racially different.

Clarence's death brought all these different people together to celebrate, and to examine their own lives. He may not have been a Sylvia Ashton-

Warner, but I am proud to be a teacher when I think about his work and his relationships with children.

Children will not only remember the songs he taught them, but his kindness, love and dedication. This confirms my belief that money is not the only factor that motivates us to return in September. Among the professions, we still remain the group oriented to helping and working well with the young. Our values do distinguish us from other professions.

The stained glass window in memory of this colleague will always be a reminder to all of us of our ability to let the colourful rays of the sun shine in on the faces of all our charges.

Children paddle their own canoes to school as there are no roads or buses on the marshlands

Teaching in the New Mainstream

By Peter Jailall, The Valleys Sr. P.S.
(*The Beacon*, December 1997)

When I started teaching in Toronto in 1970, the classrooms were uniform and predictable, the curriculum was laid out clearly and it was simple. The culture of the school was very Eurocentric.

We used to sing: "Geema I want to go, Back to Ontario…"

It was a time when prosperous Ontario was home to an established group of people who didn't mind putting up with a gentle trickle of strange new faces entering through their gates at Toronto International Airport.

We celebrated Christmas in a very big way with green and red balloons dancing in classrooms, with food and drink in abundance. It was a time when principals expected a Christmas party in each room as they moved around checking and savouring chips and shortbread cookies. Today, it is not politically or culturally correct to make a big to do about Christmas, especially in our public schools.

The festive season is called "Winter Celebrations" and it's even de-emphasized in some schools. The "good old days" are gone and the "bad new ones" are here.

In the new mainstream classroom, classes are made up of children from many different parts of the world. At The Valleys where I teach for example, children come from 61 different countries. The ethno cultural make up of some of our classrooms, challenges us to change our ways of teaching and our beliefs about how children learn.

As we teach these children, we continue to make changes in the curriculum on a day-to-day basis. Curriculum designing is an ongoing process that happens in classrooms, not in boardrooms.

It's not a common document written for Tom, Dick and Mary outside of schools. We need to use the children as resources for teaching and learning. Teaching is a learning process that requires negotiation and implementation between teacher and learner in classrooms. The new mainstream classroom is no longer a place where children come from traditional family backgrounds, a place where we celebrate Father's Day and Mother's Day. Now we talk about extended families, guardians and caregivers. The Ontario Law Reform Commission is now recommending "Registered Domestic Partners," including same sex couples. We will be required to handle this complexity of family structures and relationships in our classrooms.

In the new mainstream, we are becoming more careful and sensitive about the way we deal with gender differences. We are making sure that we choose books that portray female characters in a positive way. Our choice of books, without denying history, ought to reflect the realities of gender and racial differences.

In our democracy, discrimination against any group, no matter how insignificant in number will not be tolerated. The rights of the individual are supreme in our society and those rights must also be protected in our classrooms—a microcosm of the real world. Heritage language classes are growing like mushrooms in many Metropolitan Toronto and Peel schools. Parents may soon challenge us to pay attention to the linguistic rights of their children in the regular school day as our society becomes more and more multilingual. The debate about the equality of educational opportunity is an ongoing process. Ontario classrooms are not the same old places they used to be a few decades ago.

And as teachers we must teach in ways that are consistent with the new mainstream in our classrooms today.

Interactive teaching in the hinterland school

The Gulf War

By Peter Jailall, Queenston Drive P.S.
(The Beacon, February 1991)

"We're going to die tomorrow."
"They are going to drop a nuclear bomb."
"We're scared."

These are the voices of two girls from Mr. Crawford's class the day before war was declared. They were on the verge of tears as they sought comfort from their teacher.

"I'm scared too," replied Mr. Crawford. Then they had a class meeting to talk about their fears. Once the war was declared the next day, the discussions continued interlaced with literature and poetry dealing with war and peace.

Another girl, Lindsay, in Mrs. Roy's class, writes her own poem:

Only a Man
The world has broken into a fight,
Man has trespassed with God.
Peace has left and sin has come
Man no longer walks alone,
And freedom has no home.
The light ahead is flickering
Only a man can move ahead
And put a hand to stop the war
Only a man…

Wednesday, January 15th war broke out.

We were forced to deal with the real feelings of children. We had little time to even consider our own emotions. Our children came first. We comforted. We taught lessons. Most of us stayed neutral.

We handled the trauma of war in different, but personal ways as we continued to wait for peace. Boys tend to be more aggressive both in their writing and in their talk about the war.

Mike wrote, "Bush is going to kick butts."

It is not easy to agree publicly with Mike in a politically and culturally diverse classroom (not to mention Canada's peace-keeping role in the Gulf). It becomes extremely difficult for any teacher to support "butt-kicking" especially when we see crying children struggling to put on uncomfortable gas masks.

The sight of maimed children and bombed schools makes teachers angry even though the suffering ones may belong "on the other side." It seems to be an unwritten code in our profession not to condone or support violence. War goes against all of our daily efforts at civilizing the human race.

We detest war because we know too well the high human and financial costs. After the war, there will be a further reduction on the amount of money allocated to educating children. Money spent on the war could have been used to feed hungry children and promote knowledge and literacy both in North America and other countries.

This dangerous hi-tech war is an eye-opener to us educators. It has made us more vigilant as we further examine the double role science and technology can play in schools and in research centres. What is the purpose of promoting science and on spending heavily on technology when this knowledge is being used for human destruction? It seems as if Research and Development in science and technology since Vietnam had been gearing up, preparing a complex, insidious war machine bent on mass killing, pollution and air destruction. Sometimes we feel helpless and powerless. Our leaders give orders to make weapons and we follow silently.

What new discoveries have been made in the health sciences? What efforts have been made to alleviate poverty? Instead of using the money and knowledge in technology to clean up the environment, we are engaging in a war that is further destroying the earth.

As the war wages on, we are witnessing two wars—one in Iraq and one on our T.V. screens. The one in Iraq is the real one where lives, property and relationships are destroyed daily. And we know no one will win. The war on the T.V. screen—the battle for our minds, is the artificial Nintendo war that numbs and hides the real hideous deformity. The media have transformed us all into passive spectators. Our children (especially the boys) have been fully prepared even before the war, practising their launches during their play at Nintendo games. Now, they are selling the war to us in the same manner in which they sold Nintendo games to our children. But we don't have to buy it.

Yes, the war continues like wars that have been waged before. At one time Rome was the centre of the universe with its military columns, its gladiators and its equestrian teams. Rome fell. Then Britannia ruled the waves. Today America rules the skies. Tomorrow, when America falls, some other nation or group of nations will rise up, usurp power and fight for a dominant place in the world order. There will never be any permanent peace in human societies. Our human imperfections do not permit utopia on earth. There will continue to be more dirty little wars around after this "mother of all wars" is over.

War mongers and peacemakers come and go. Peacemakers though, remain the salt of the earth. The very nature of our profession makes us peacemakers. We continue to add flavour to each generation whenever there seems to be little hope. And we continue comforting children in distress.

Whole-Language and Multiculturalism in Grades One and Two

By Prof. Robert P. Parker, University of La Verne California and Peter Jailall
(Ontario Council of Teachers of English Indirections, January 1994)

But if there are all sorts of children together, having a range of skills, cultures, backgrounds, origins, languages, dialects, perceptions, experiences, fears, hopes, aspirations, joys...then the possibilities for exciting interactions over a story are as infinite as the stars...

That's how it was with the children I taught. They made rich stories. And while making those stories together, they made friendships. And they made peace. And none of it was nonsense. (Betty Rosen, 1988)

For decades, but especially since the end of World War II, people from all over the world have immigrated to North America: from many different Asian countries; from Lebanon and other parts of the Middle East; from Eastern Europe; from the former Yugoslavia; from El Salvador and Nicaragua; from Mexico; from various African countries; from Portugal; from India and Pakistan; from Sri Lanka; and from many others. Some flee repression and persecution in their homelands, while some flee famine or civil war, or both. Nearly all seek increased economic opportunities and a better life for themselves and their children. They, also, make significant, sometimes wrenching and painful, adjustments— cultural, social, and often linguistic. Sometimes these adjustments require the adults and their children to make great personal sacrifices.

Most parents encourage their children to learn English so that they may succeed academically and economically in their adopted country. Nonetheless, public schools are often the first place where immigrant children encounter a new culture as well as a new language. Fortunately, materials are available to help educators teach new immigrant children to become literate in English. Many teachers work hard to help these children learn to speak and read English; however, relatively few teachers emphasize learning to write in English. Even fewer, though, encourage children from widely different cultural and linguistic backgrounds to use writing as a primary vehicle for learning English or for constructing knowledge, building stronger self-concepts, and developing inter-cultural understanding.

In urban areas all across North America, public school classrooms reflect the rapidly growing cultural, racial, linguistic and religious diversity of the

U.S. and Canada. In some schools in the Toronto area, for example, children come speaking forty or more different native languages, and Toronto is not alone among North American cities in this regard. For some schools, this challenging social-linguistic situation is complicated by the arrival of children from places like Bosnia and Somalia and Rumania. Beyond the dislocation of moving to a new country, many of these children are experiencing the trauma resulting from extraordinary loss and deprivation. So, the difficulties teachers in these schools face in their efforts to educate children extend beyond the already challenging barriers created by linguistic, cultural, racial and ethnic differences.

Our story is about one such classroom, in McBride Public School in Mississauga, Ontario: the years are 1987-1989. During the first of these two years, Peter taught a combined Grade 1/2 class, and during the second, a Grade 2 class. All the children in this story were between the ages of six and eight. Both classes reflected great cultural and linguistic diversity. The following languages were spoken, read, and written in their homes: Chinese (Mandarin and Cantonese), Arabic (two kinds), Greek, Urdu, Hindi, Punjabi, Italian, Vietnamese, Koran, Portuguese, English, and West Indian dialect (English-based). Today, these classes would be even more culturally and linguistically diverse.

In their homes, many parents, and children, wrote both in English and in their various native languages. For household as well as for business purposes, many families made lists, wrote directions and instructions, wrote notes, wrote cards to celebrate religious and other holidays, and so forth. Sometimes children helped their parents to gather needed information in English, and sometimes they also helped their parents to translate this information into the family's native tongue—or vice versa. Sometimes, parents and children together wrote long letters to relatives or friends still living in their native country. And sometimes the parents read religious books to the family: the Koran, the Bhagavad Gita, the Bible, and so on. Typically, these books were written in the family's native language, not in English.

The children worshipped in Moslem mosques, in Hindu and Sikh temples, and in many different Christian churches. Some of the services they attended were conducted in native tongues and some in English. On Saturdays many children attended heritage language classes where they studied the family's native language and used both it and English to communicate. Many children had grandparents living with them who spoke only the family's native language. More than half the children from each year's class watched both English language and native language TV programs and listened to the same variety of radio programs. So, many of these children were involved almost constantly in bilingual, even trilingual, situations.

Classrooms like these two are the "new mainstream" in North America, especially in our cities. More and more classrooms every day reflect the kind of multicultural bringing together which characterized Peter's classroom. And for him, as for thousands of other teachers across North America, this bringing together of children from such diverse backgrounds, in a country whose language and culture is new if not foreign to many of them, creates both problems and possibilities. The problems are philosophical, curricular, and pedagogical as well as, in a broader but no less pressing sense, political, economic and religious. The possibilities are the same. In order to teach this "new mainstream" of children successfully, Peter—and teachers like him—must examine both their curriculum and their method of teaching. Implicitly or explicitly, they must address questions like the following:

- How might the children's cultural, linguistic, religious, and racial differences most productively be viewed?
- Should these differences be viewed as barriers to effective instruction or as resources to be incorporated and used to expand learning and growth?
- Should children be changed to fit the traditional curriculum and instructional techniques, or should both curriculum and instruction be changed to fit the children?
- Should children's differences, especially by those in power, be viewed as a threat to current values and power relationships, or should these differences be viewed as offering rich possibilities for cultural renewal and transformation?

Though these questions are as fundamentally political as they are educational, we will address only their curricular and pedagogical implications, leaving aside the political dimensions for the time being. For us, the principal question is: How can the increasing multicultural diversity of our school populations be used as rich, new resource for creating intercultural classrooms? By intercultural classrooms, we mean classrooms in which the values and structures support children in developing intercultural understanding and relationships, experiencing each other in the fullness and richness of their diversity, and learning from this experience in lifelong ways.

Peter, himself an immigrant, values every child's background and culture and includes all of them centrally in the classroom curriculum process (Burgess, 1988)—from the white, fourth generation "Canadian" boy to the girl who arrived the day before from Portugal. He encourages the development of a learning conversation which includes and uses every child's experiences, knowledge, values, perspectives, and languages. The classroom curriculum process (i.e. all of what actually happens in the classroom on a daily basis, not just the written curriculum of the school or Peter's lesson plans) expands constantly to incorporate what the children know and value, as well as what they imagine and wonder about and wish for.

Obviously, much of the children's exchange of cultural/linguistic experience and knowledge takes place through the talking, reading, drawing, and drama they do, but their writing, in Peter's classroom, constitutes perhaps the most powerful means of creating a curriculum process characterized by genuine intercultural communication and learning. Peter consciously organizes his classroom to promote intercultural relationships, collaboration, and understanding. He works to create a context which invites the exchange and examination of the range of interesting and illuminating cultural, linguistic, and religious knowledge and practices which the children bring with them.

During these two years, the children in Peter's classroom wrote, on average, for 45-60 minutes each morning. Every child wrote something during that time, regardless of ability or interest. All wrote about whatever they wanted to, or were able to, using their available linguistic resources. Many returned to their writing at times during the day when they weren't engaged in other work.

Some took their writing to the schoolyard at recess; some wrote on the school bus; and some wrote at home, alone or in collaboration with siblings, parents, relatives, or peers. Some children got together on weekends to play and spent some of their time writing.

So, while "writing workshop" occurred officially each morning in Peter's classroom, it also occurred unofficially at many other times and in many other places.

During "writing workshop" children sometimes wrote alone and sometimes with self-chosen partners. The writing "partnerships" seldom numbered more than three children, though occasionally they were larger. Children wrote at their desks, on the floor, at easels, and in the hallway. For nearly an hour, the classroom became a "writing place" for the children—more like a studio in structure than like a classroom. Children wrote at their own pace and at their own "level" of communicative competence. They wrote about personal experiences, what they were reading, and what they experienced outside the school. Children who had difficulty writing in English wrote in their native languages or combined English words with their native tongue. Sometimes Peter encouraged a child struggling with English to write with a more fluent partner, but only when he thought the child could accept this suggestion without insult.

The children chose both topics and forms. Peter assigned neither, nor did he ever correct or otherwise evaluate any piece of writing. Instead, Peter valued each piece of writing, regardless of topic, length, fluency, or any other quality, modelling this response for the children. Each child was taken seriously as a writer who could make interesting pieces of writing for others to hear and read, though some efforts were acknowledged to be more successful than others.

Each day children read their writing aloud during various kinds of "readarounds": sometimes the audience was a small, spontaneously assembled group, and sometimes it was the entire class. During the "readarounds" children gave their personal responses to each piece or asked questions of the writer. Peter intervened judiciously, always in a low key way and only when absolutely necessary to maintain attention to the piece or respect for the writer.

Writing sessions in classrooms like Peter's have been well documented in the literature on "process" writing and "whole language." Beginning in the U.K. with the work of the Rosens (Rosen and Rosen, 1973) and continuing on through such publications as *Understanding Children's Writing* (Martin et al, 1976), the work of Graves (1983) and Calkins (1983; 1986), of the Goodmans (1991; 1986; 1988), of Nancy Atwell (1991; 1987; 1989), and of the many others who have rushed into the field of "whole language" instruction, often with hardly an historical or theoretical glance around, the pedagogy of "process" writing has been laid out in detail. Much of this literature emphasizes learning to write rather than writing to learn. The "process" approach is presented as a means, a technology, to achieve the end of improved writing. After enough years of process writing or whole language classrooms, Johnny will be able to write—whatever that might mean to those who assiduously detail the technology while begging this more fundamental question.

Our purpose in telling this "story" about Peter's classroom, though, is not to add new wrinkles to the "technology" or process writing, nor is it to discuss the ways in which Peter's "writing workshop" differs from the technology of orthodox process writing classrooms. Rather, we are interested in the ways in which doing writing—in certain ways under certain conditions, and across cultural, racial, linguistic, and religious differences—leads children to collaborate, to form personal relationships, to achieve new interpersonal understanding, as well as to learn about language and writing. We want to understand more about how "process" writing, done in a knowledgeably skillful way, serves as a means to an end beyond improvement in writing skill. This end, in fact, is the growth of persons, and improvement in writing skill is a by-product of the collaboration, the new understandings, and the developing relationships which lead to this end. In our judgement, children's skill in writing improves more substantially when such improvement is not the primary goal, occurring rather as a result of more socially meaningful interactions and activities and growth. Writing to get better at writing produces less satisfactory results than writing to get better at living.

As Harold Rosen observed:

It would seem, then, that nothing need change. The tried and true recipe, good reading and good writing, makes unnecessary any concessions to multicultural education. What is this good writing and good reading which can be conjured out of processes which have nothing to do with the lived culture of the children? (1982, 14)

In fact, as Peter's classroom illustrates, the source of good writing and good reading, when they occur, is always the "lived culture of the children." Other sorts of writing and reading, no matter how "good" they appear or what test scores they produce, are illusions rather than the real thing. Children's lived culture is the only source of writing and reading which makes a genuine and lasting difference in their development as attentive, open-minded, whole-hearted, responsible persons and as lifelong writers and readers.

Gradually, as children participate in writing situations (and other situations as well) which value, draw on, and incorporate their lived culture, they become a community. But they become more than a community of writers. They become a community of learners formed by writing, especially as the writing occasions intercultural communication and learning. In effect, writing helps these children join Peter in creating significant contexts: contexts highlighted by their use of writing to "pool" their knowledge and ideas about themselves and the world, to express their feelings and personal responses to experience, and to reach beyond the bounds of the classroom and school to share their work (and themselves) with a wider world of teachers, parents, friends, and siblings.

During holidays, especially summer, many of Peter's children revisited their countries of origin, bringing back interesting experiences and artifacts. They shared their experiences and some of the artifacts with each other, and they wrote about the experiences as well.

Sylvia, age 7, wrote:

Last Thursday, I went to Egypt. It was fun there, but I keep on getting allergies on my skin. There are many cats on the street and they can bite you.
I spent two days in Cairo at my Aunt's house.
Egypt and Cairo are opiasites.
I am going to write some Egyptian words.

Egypt		Cairo
ahlen	—	hello
ah	—	yes
laa	—	no
cockren	—	thank you
hamar	—	donkey
hosan	—	horse
akle	—	food
roh	—	go

Sylvia also brought back Egyptian artifacts, and she became the class authority on Egypt. During the "readaround," she taught the class all she knew about the geography and history of Egypt and introduced her classmates to some Egyptian vocabulary. After this session, a small group of children from the class decided to work with Sylvia to find out more about Egypt. None were of Egyptian background, so this was truly a new experience for them. They visited Sylvia's home to see some of the more valuable artifacts that she was not permitted to bring to school, and they shared their experiences with the rest of the class. In this way, Sylvia's initial writing about Egypt, shared during the "readaround," became a vehicle that, with Peter's support, led to extended learning about Egypt for the class, to new personal relationships, and to deepened intercultural understanding and collaboration among the children.

Sophia was born in India. She decided to write in a different language script with English subtitles in order to show her friends something about India. Thus, she introduced the Hindi script system to the class. She wrote about the climate—"India is hot"— and she showed the class where India is on the world map. Gurdeep Singh, a Sikh from the Punjab who also was born in India, wrote about the Sikh religion: "Sikhs should have five special things to show that they are Sikhs." Later, Gurdeep explained the meaning of the "five special things" to the class. Gurdeep's writing, together with his class discussion, not only conveyed information about the Sikh religion to his classmates but also taught understanding and tolerance at a time when anti-Sikh feelings were running high in Canada. By easing racial/religious tensions in the classroom, Gurdeep contributed in a small way to easing such tensions in the wider community.

Maurice and Carlton, both of Afro-Caribbean background, worked together to compose a rap. First, they composed it orally, and then they wrote it down.

The transit, the transit
The transit's on strike We don't need no transit
'Cause we're goin' to ride our bikes.

Influenced by the development of rap among young Afro-Americans, and becoming comfortable enough with their classmates, they used their vernacular English to comment on a recent transit strike by city workers. They understood that both vernacular English and a pop music form would be accepted in their classroom, so they could use both to make a humorous political statement.

Melissa, an Anglo-Canadian whose great-grandparents came to Canada more than a hundred years ago, wrote about a wedding she attended.

"On Saturday, September 24th I went to a wedding. It was my uncle's wedding. We drove to Owen Sound where we stayed in a motel. After the wedding, they cleared the room to dance. Sabrine and I asked the D.J. if he could play the Bird Dance."

When Melissa read her piece aloud to the class, a few children new to Canada asked her to explain the bird dance. A lively discussion followed about dances from other cultures around the world. Finally, Melissa demonstrated the bird dance, including all the other children who didn't know about it in her demonstration.

At one and the same time, Melissa shared aspects of her culture and folklore with more recent Canadians for whom this knowledge was all new, and she learned new things herself about other children's culture and folklore.

Like Melissa, Kerri's roots went back over one hundred years in Canada. When some children from other, very different cultures, refused to believe her story about the "Tooth Fairy," she got quite upset. In response to their disbelief, Kerri wrote:

A long time ago, my tooth started to get loose and I did not want anyone to touch it. I did not feel good because I could not eat an apple … Then I pulled it out. That night I showed my Mom and then I went to bed. I put my tooth under my pillow. The tooth fairy came. In the morning I looked under my pillow and I saw two dollars. Some people do not believe in the tooth fairy, but I do …

Melissa and Kerri, two Anglo-Canadian children, shared part of their roots—their history and culture—with their classmates, many of whom had recently immigrated to Canada. Their classmates' curiosity about the Bird Dance and disbelief about the tooth fairy opened the way for mutual exchange and learning. As the children swapped stories, myths, and folklore, they learned more about each other and they became better friends.

Julia, who had recently arrived from England, teamed with Yuki, a new immigrant from Japan who spoke no English. Yuki taught Julia and a few other children some Japanese words. In return, they all taught Yuki English. Through these exchanges Yuki learned English, which was important for her, but of great importance also was the respect and appreciation the children developed for languages and cultures different from their own. They drew two conclusions: (1) English is not the only language in the world, and (2) Japanese script was impossible for them to understand. From the same experience, Julia discovered variations in the speech of native English speakers, and, on her own, she made a list of words that are used differently in England and Canada:

            copper   —   policeman
            coco   —   chocolate
            loo   —   washroom
            sweetie —   candy

"Writing workshop" in Peter's classroom complements the ESL program in the school. Elena arrived from Portugal in late January speaking no English at all. She could, though, write some Portuguese. Peter teamed her with Debbie, who was bilingual in English and Portuguese.

On her first day in school, from watching the other children and being coached by them, Elena got the "idea" of writing time and began to draw and to write in Portuguese. Then, one day, with no pressure from Peter, she began to label her drawings in English. She asked Peter to write the words in English, and she copied them. Her first written words in English were sun, clouds, tree, and grass. After a few more days, she drew pictures of her friends and "wrote" their names herself by using the first letter of their names (and, in two instances, two letters).

Elena's classmates consistently supported her efforts to speak and write in English. They coached her on what to do when, showed her how to say and write things in English, praised her efforts, and generally assisted her in adapting socially and linguistically within the classroom. As a result, Elena experienced no cultural or linguistic isolation whatsoever. Instead, because her classmates accepted her and recognized her abilities, needs, and experiences, she formed friendships, got on with her class work, and learned to speak English quite well within four months of her arrival. In effect, her classmates were her most successful ESL instructors, even though she attended a formal ESL class for forty minutes daily.

Other teachers and students at McBride Public School often referred to Peter as the "writing man." And, obviously, writing was important to Peter and played a central role in his classroom. Nonetheless, writing was not the most important or valued activity, not even during "writing workshop" time, nor was development in the children's writing abilities the primary goal. Writing was, rather, what we would call a pivotal activity in Peter's classroom and the focal point of the children's "effortful play" (Spencer, 1986). This effortful play, which included talking, reading, drawing and doing drama as well as writing, was the children's work, and this work was the source of their learning and development.

Peter carefully avoided teaching these children the lesson that most children learn too well and too permanently from their primary grade experience: that writing and reading are arduous, unpleasant, externally-mandated work. So Peter's students construed writing, reading, drawing, and doing drama as pleasurable activities: ones that they could choose, direct, and evaluate themselves. And, quite predictably, they approached these activities enthusiastically, energetically, and imaginatively, with no reluctance or hesitation.

There was, in Peter's classroom, scope for the children's intentions to operate in generating and directing their writing, reading, drawing and dramatic "work"—including scope for choosing when to work with a partner and whom that partner would be. Allowing scope for children's intentions leads, as Nancy Martin has documented (1983; 1980), to a commitment on the children's parts to relationships and to learning. The evidence of such a commitment was obvious to even the most casual observer of Peter's classroom. Moreover, by allowing scope for children's intentions to be enacted and therefore, incorporated into the classroom curriculum process, Peter also allowed scope for children's prior knowledge of many matters, from literacy to the customs of their native lands to be incorporated into that same process. "Curriculum negotiation" occurred virtually every day (Boomer, 1982).

Literacy instruction in many classrooms has "a narrowing effect" (Spencer, 1986) on children's learning, but not here. Here, because they could choose the material and the forms and the partnerships for their writing and reading work, and because doing the work involved them in meaningful intercultural exchanges, children's literacy experiences had "an expanding effect" on their learning. Crucially, Peter saw this scope for intentions, for choice, and for intercultural exchange as lying at the heart of the classroom curriculum process. Children's learning of language skills was not the heart of the matter for him; children using language to grow in understanding, judgement, and responsibility was.

In Peter's classroom, children talked, wrote, read, drew and did drama every day, and they experienced their social interactions and processes of doing this work as valued equally with their work products. Through what they valued and what they did, Peter and the children, in collaboration, created a context for significant experiences and learning. Moreover, Peter never subsumed the children's lives (see Denison, 1968) beneath the overarching concern that his school and so many others display for the evaluation of products and outcomes. That is, Peter preserved the integrity of classroom relationships and learning by organizing the conditions of his classroom (Dewey, 1963) primarily to educate children and only secondarily to evaluate them. He refused to let his attention be diverted from the children's interactions, work, and learning by the pressure to reduce these human matters to a narrow range of evaluative judgements, so correspondingly the children's attention was not diverted from their work to their teacher's judgements about them.

Though we think these conclusions about Peter's classroom are valid and important, they do not take us deep enough into the complex issues which we must confront. It is important to be able to say, "Yes, children's literacy abilities do develop rapidly in this kind of context through this kind of curriculum process," and, "Yes, they do develop in important ways through their literacy experiences," and "Yes, their literacy learning and their overall personal growth are important." Many people may take this story to be both sufficient and complete in itself, but for us this is only part of the story. While Peter's classroom, as context, was significant in its support of children's literacy learning and of their personal growth, his classroom was even more significant in its creation of a democratic social and intellectual experience for every child.

Peter's classroom, we claim, was democratic in the most powerful and valuable sense of the term. "A democracy," Dewey (1966) said, "is more than a form of government; it is primarily a mode of associated living, of conjoint communicated experience." The children in Peter's class didn't just "do school" in the sense of completing the assigned work individually and competitively, and they didn't just learn "skills," so they didn't recreate the anti-democratic hierarchy which most schools maintain through streaming, explicit and implicit, and through comparative grading.

Rather, they participated in "a mode of associated living," of living more and more together in their classroom community. They communicated about their experience, past and present, drawing each other into their individual cultures and values and, thus, creating a new culture of the classroom with the resources of their collective cultures and imaginations. They engaged in the democratic process of reconstructing culture rather than simply or passively receiving cultural transmissions.

Desirable democratic experience, Dewey also said, has two important elements. One is the "recognition of mutual interests as a factor in social control," and the other is "freer interaction among social groups," resulting in the "breaking down of those barriers of class, race…which keep [people] from perceiving the full import of their activity" (1966). Certainly, these children recognized and pursued their mutual interests. One day, for example, when Bob was visiting Peter's class, he noticed two boys (one white and one black) in a corner working at a large easel. When he asked them what they were doing, they said they were writing a story, with pictures, on "black holes" in space. They had seen a television program on this topic and had talked a little with Peter about "black holes," and they wanted to make something to express their interest and to use their evolving knowledge. These seven year old boys, from families of limited education and means, were capable of developing an interest in, and knowledge about, a quite sophisticated topic and of sharing their learning with their classmates through writing and illustrating a story.

Certainly, also, these children broke down racial and cultural barriers through their free interactions with each other and through the inter-racial and inter-cultural friendships they formed: three girls talking and writing together, one from Guyana (Afro-Caribbean), one from Portugal, and one from Yugoslavia (white); or two girls doing a play together, one from India (South Asian) and one from Portugal; or two boys writing together, one from Taiwan (Chinese) and one from Jamaica (Afro-Caribbean).

These democratic values, it is essential to understand, cannot be treated or posed as curricular goals. They are not outcomes to be achieved, not ends in themselves, but ways of being—qualities of the interactions among individuals in particular settings—which either can be said to characterize the social processes in these settings or not. In each particular setting and situation, people interact with each other, and the process of their interactions is characterized by a democratic quality or it isn't. The same is true of classrooms. The curriculum process in a given classroom is either democratic or it isn't. When children experience a democratic classroom curriculum process, they learn democracy; when they experience an autocratic or elitist or racist classroom curriculum process, they learn these values. Children learn what they experience and practice.

Peter consciously organizes his classroom to support a democratic curriculum process. Children who experience this kind of curriculum process develop and pursue their own interests and goals, work together supportively and collaboratively, form relationships, and learn of and from this process. This curriculum process, and the context for significant learning it creates, serves the children as a source of "liberation of a greater diversity of personal capacities" (Dewey, 1966). Through this greater diversity of capacities, children create a culture, and they then interact with this culture to further liberate an even more diverse range of capacities. And this culture-making is more than timely at this point in the history of North America; it is essential if we are, as William Faulkner said, to prevail rather than just to survive.

Building Collegiality Through Storytelling

By Peter Jailall, The Valleys Sr. P.S.

On November 15, Fairview Public School celebrated a full day of *Books and Storytelling*. The regular academic program was suspended, permitting educators from near and far to work together in a big storytelling extravaganza.

Classroom teachers, resource teachers, consultants, and even the superintendent came out to tell stories. Teachers worked in teams telling stories to full classes, sometimes getting the students to do follow-up activities. The students enjoyed the diversity of the stories, the different teaching styles and the rich cultural swapping. It was a unique experience, using stories as vehicles in the teaching-learning process. The students were actively involved in chants, choral reading, listening, singing, picture making, and drama. It was a successful learning experience for both the students and the teachers.

The Fairview event was a good demonstration of what collegiality is all about. The teachers were involved in joint planning to organize the day's activities. Letters of invitation were sent out to the storytellers. Food was catered in. Work was done jointly to co-ordinate time and space. On the whole, a generosity of spirit prevailed among staff members, leading to a most successful enterprise.

Team teaching took place during the sessions and mentor relationships were built. Together, teachers were building a collaborative culture, and one that was voluntary. It was fun to be engaged in work that produced results. Teachers were eager to cover classes, provide materials, share tasks, and just generally look out for one another. It was a time of teachers helping teachers, not one of contrived collegiality. The day saw a significant move away from traditional teacher solitude, from the teacher as a "shut-in," alone in a room with a class of children, chiselling away at her own sculpture.

As a professional body, we have been conditioned to sit and chip away at our own marble, aloof from our colleagues. It's time we give other teachers permission to join us in sculpting the model. Joint work in storytelling, on that November day at Fairview, helped us to break through the restraints of teacher individualism and isolationism, even if it were just for the day.

During the lunch hour and at recess, teachers talked freely and with excitement about the experience. There was talk in the hallway, talk in the library, talk in the staff-room, and even talk in the parking lot. Teachers asked questions of each other: How did it go? What story did you tell? Are you going to tell the same one again? Was there much class participation? What did you do for a follow-up? This was teacher talk with a purpose. And, in the process of asking questions for clarification, telling success stories, and savouring the joys of the day, teachers were cutting down on the intellectual, emotional and social demands of the job.

This kind of teamwork had an underlying structure that encouraged interdependence among colleagues. As well, it was an excellent model for the students as they watched us collaborating, sharing knowledge and problem solving together. It was professional development at its best.

The research on collegiality concludes that there are many benefits when teachers are engaged in "joint work." There is an increased commitment to continue learning at home. Teachers themselves benefit from "joint work." They feel supported, successful and satisfied, reaping the rewards of teaching together.

In a hospital, doctors, nurses, social workers, clergy and kitchen staff work together as a team to save lives. The Fairview experience is surely testimony to the idea that the educational staff can also band together as a team to save lives in our schools.

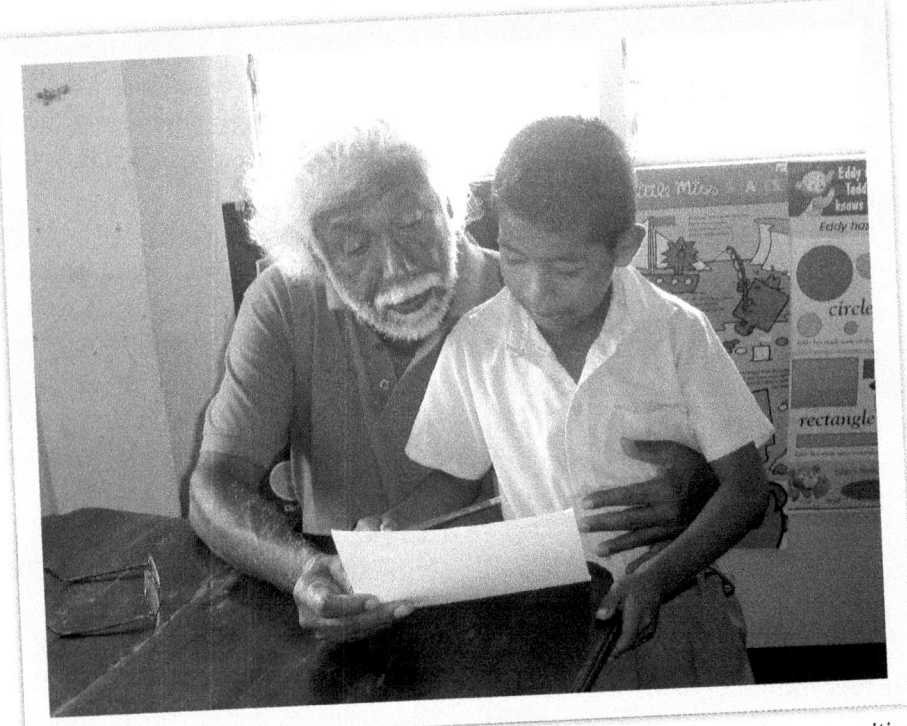

Helping a shy student correct his own writing

Writing Empowers ESL/ESD Learners: Case of Winnie (Age 6)

By Peter Jailall, Queenston Drive P.S.

(*The Beacon*, May 1991)

Winnie, a quiet, shy grade one ESL student was admitted to Queenston Drive P.S. in September 1990. She did not utter a word to me or to her classroom teacher, Ms. Thurston for three months. We were beginning to worry, but we waited.

On October 8th, Winnie printed her name—Winnie, then she drew a picture to represent herself. During November and December, she used picture making to represent significant others in her life—her mother, father, sister and friend.

I worked with Winnie, talking to her about her pictures, her family, her friends. At the same time I helped her label her pictures and provided opportunities for her to share her work with others.

All along she was always free to set her own agenda about what she wanted to draw and label. I intervened judiciously. She drew and we labeled together—the sun, house, ice-cream, tree, book and pizza.

In January and February 1991, I continued coaching and supporting her in her writing endeavours. After the completion of each piece of writing and artwork, I praised Winnie for her efforts which I valued very much. I also had confidence in her ability to create pieces of writing. I exercised patience and praised her small efforts.

She worked within a community of other primary writers as they supported each other talking about pictures, ideas and the possible spelling of words. They giggled as they exchanged their own linguistic scripts with each other. During this process of sharing, they came to understand that they each had their own unique form of writing—Cantonese, Japanese, Portuguese, Punjabi and Hindi. I permitted them to write and talk both in English and in their mother tongue.

It was mid-April 1991, when Winnie suddenly started to put words together to make meaning in her own simple way. She wrote:

"I like my mother to me. I like my father to me. I like my sister to me. I like Kyoko (her friend) to me."

She was now making and reading longer texts in English and in Cantonese. She began to share her pieces of writing with her classmates in

ESL and in her homeroom. She also shared with her parents on "Parents' Night." She was now hooked on drawing, writing, reading and talking about her work. She "blossomed," as teachers would say. She discovered the joy of sharing with others. But most of all, she suddenly found out how writing could make others listen, respond and recognize her.

She became a new student—talking, laughing, enjoying school, making friends, learning language skills and gaining confidence to launch out further afield into other areas of the curriculum.

Winnie continues to acquire new knowledge every day in her drawing, writing, reading and talking. And she is doing it all by herself with full support from her classmates and me. She has been truly empowered through her own writing and thinking.

Singing and making friends—school is fun!

Suffer the Little Children

By Peter Jailall, McBride Avenue P.S.

(*The Beacon*, September 1988)

We will receive them in September—these innocent, intelligent and willing-to-learn, young pre-schoolers. And we are ready!

Many teachers are storming into principals' offices, anxiously requesting to teach them. Many senior administrators are working hard to help them make the transition from their quiet homes to our busy schools less traumatic. Many parents can't wait to shoo them away from their favourite American cartoon shows.

Our preparation for them has already opened up the debate about some burning educational issues—educational costs, physical space, bussing, safety, time management, learning theories and school-community relations. Their presence in our schools will certainly force us to examine more carefully how very young children acquire knowledge. And these four-year-olds do have a lot to teach us. Forget this business that we will be running a babysitting service.

These children have already had four years of learning in their world and they have acquired all kinds of skills and knowledge—in language acquisition, in science and in math. Many will come to us knowing their colours. They are at a prime stage in their childhood development to start learning to read, to write and to socialize. They have been reading words and messages from the refrigerator doors in their kitchens. They have been reading environmental print in our shopping malls and T.V. screens. Many of them have been listening to their parents telling or reading stories to them. Some of them have been attending Sunday schools where they have experienced a rich language learning environment.

These junior kindergarten children have seen their moms or dads writing shopping lists, filling out catalogue forms and signing cheques. They are ready to "sign" themselves in on that first September morning for us to teach them.

What can we teach them? Research tells us that they are ready to read and write, even at that tender age, and so we need to provide a climate in their classrooms that will encourage more opportunities for language acquisition. We will read to them regularly and we will encourage them to write as they engage in picture making, painting and play. We will also help them to "label" things around the classroom.

At their age they have this burning urge to tell, and so we will be listening attentively to them as they tell us stories about their young lives. In turn, we will mesmerize them with our skills in storytelling. We will encourage drama, puppetry and miming to extend their imagination.

We will guide them to engage in symbolic and parallel play, and all the other kinds of play that we read about in educational textbooks.

The play-way method of acquiring knowledge and social skills will be strongly emphasized in their curriculum. Play materials need not be expensive. Young children delight in manipulating, examining, building and destroying "junk" materials that are inexpensive and easily accessible in the world at large. Also, they enjoy bonding with each other as they make friends in their social relationships—a sadly neglected area in the curriculum of the young. School is the best environment for these youngsters, if only to give them an opportunity to be with other children, to stretch the different strands of their personalities as they dialogue with their peers.

They will certainly be very active, requiring a well-thought-out physical and health education program that must include movements in dance and circle games. Then, after all, what good is physical activity without a rest period and snack time? This will be an excellent opportunity for them to learn more social skills at the table.

We will not only emphasize the academics at this early stage, but we will be starting them off right with essential life skills. And we have good teachers among us who are ready — professionals with knowledge, skills and experience. They also have a love for little children, an essential ingredient in moulding the lives of our future generation in Peel.

> "At their age they have this burning urge to tell, and so we will be listening attentively to them as they tell us stories about their young lives. In turn, we will mesmerize them with our skills in storytelling. We will encourage drama, puppetry and miming to extend their imagination."

T'is the Season

By Peter Jailall, McBride Avenue P.S.
(*The Beacon*, December 1987)

Recently I was part of a team of teachers in my school planning a theme together for the winter months. The theme, "Festivals Around the World," was chosen instead of the traditional "Christmas Around the World." The focus of the planning session was to give students and their parents an opportunity to become resource people to the school, sharing their own religious and cultural festivals. This also made them feel a part of the planning process.

I have used the theme "Christmas Around the World" for many years, and indeed it was a relevant theme to the majority of students under my charge due to the strong monocultural nature of our society at that time. I have chosen Christmas greetings in many languages where Christmas as a religious custom is celebrated—"Meilleurs Voeux" and "Felices Fiestas." I have also explored the different names given to Santa Claus, like Pere Noel and Father Christmas.

I have even pointed out that, in the Caribbean, we have our own black Santa Claus on parade. In that sunshine climate, we celebrate Christmas from mid-November to mid-January with our colourful parades, carolling, exchanging of gifts and drinking bottles of rum. People from all races and creeds join in the celebrations. Many Caribbean people here are a bit disappointed at the brevity of the festive season.

I think Canadian schools are the only places where we celebrate the festive season for the longest period of time. And by celebration I mean the music, singing, academic work, exchanging of gifts and sharing of treats—the whole mood of joy and laughter that permeates our school halls and our gymnasiums.

But, more than before, I am becoming aware of the growing number of non-Christian children in our schools—children who are not permitted to celebrate Christmas because it is not their religious holiday. Mind you, I don't believe that many of us are engaged in a religious celebration at Christmas time. To me it is a mere indulgence in that aspect of western materialism that is decadent.

As a teacher I can rationalize with a group of adults by sending them off to work quietly in the library or in the hallway, but with children it is different. It is hard for me to deal with a non-participating group or an individual child sitting in a corner feeling left out, rejected or sad. It is difficult for me to handle this kind of religious segregation in a public school.

The Christian children are too young to understand the aloofness of their friends. They will share their treats lovingly and willingly with their non-Christian classmates who will accept reluctantly. Then there I am feeling guilty, sending them off to another place in the school, treating them differently when we sing religious carols.

I wonder sometimes about teaching in a public education system—a system that is also quietly and strongly Judeo-Christian in its cultural values, yet trying to accommodate all irrespective of religious beliefs. We as a public education system do not have the right to impose our concept of the good in religious matters. Do we view Christmas as a secular celebration, a religious celebration or just the change of a season? If our mandate concerning the public role of the school is to promote good citizenship and a sense of justice and equality, then we have no right to encroach on children's fundamental, private convictions. We would be more in tune with the nature of our clientele if we avoid these private matters, i.e. religious celebrations, and concentrate on neutral or collective ways of celebrating to include all children.

My colleagues and I, together with some parents and their children, have already embarked on the theme, "Festivals Around the World," a theme that will last until February.

We may eventually decide to do the theme all year, starting next September. In this way we will include in our celebration Chinese New Year, Jewish Chanukah, the Muslim Eid, the Hindu Diwali and the Christian Christmas (we will send the atheists to the office). I know that Christmas is the special event in our culture, and any attempt to change it around will raise high emotions.

But later we may have to settle to keep it out of our public schools or celebrate it with other religious festivals.

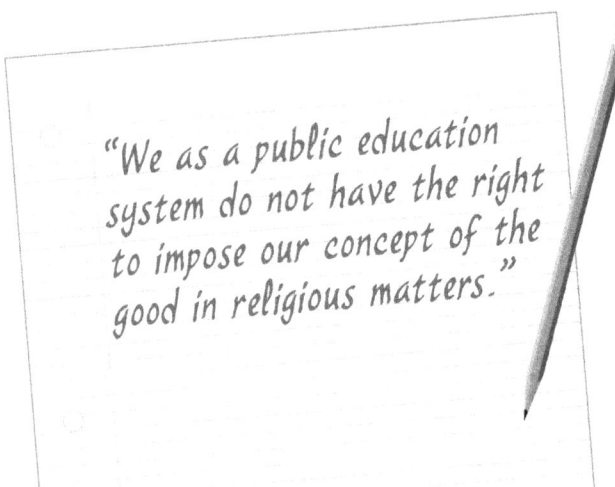

"We as a public education system do not have the right to impose our concept of the good in religious matters."

Our Father ...?

By Peter Jailall, McBride Avenue P.S.

"We were talking about the significance of the Lord's Prayer in school last week, when one of my teaching colleagues declared passionately: "Why do they want to change our tradition around? If I go to Saudi Arabia, I will have to conform to their way of doing things. Why do I have to bend over backwards to accommodate newcomers?"

The Lord's Prayer is a sacred cow to many Canadians living in the Region of Peel. The Ontario Court of Appeal's decision to ban the prayer from public schools has made many parents angry. Some Peel parents felt so strongly about this issue that they went to the Board to lodge their protests. They felt that their rights as Christians have been violated and that Judeo-Christian ideals have been sacrificed to multiculturalism.

Consequently, the trustees of the Peel Board appealed the Court's decision. Will the Court of Appeal reverse its decision? If not, what can we as educators do in order to come to some compromise when dealing with such an emotional issue?

Here are five options to consider:

Option I: We break the law of Caesar, and continue to obey the law of God, by saying the Lord's Prayer in our public schools without considering the religious beliefs and rights of non-Christian children and their parents.

Option II: As an educational body we compose our own universal prayer to meet the religious needs of all children. For example, we may choose to address God as Great Spirit, Mother/Father, and put atheists to stand in the hall.

Option III: We try to please everyone by having each religious group say its own prayers in different parts of the school under the guidance of a religious leader. For example, the Catholic priest will say mass with the Catholic children attending the public school; the Hindu priest will recite mantras with the Hindu children; the Muslim maulana will read namaz with the Muslim children, while the Protestant pastor will lead his flock in prayer in the gym.

Option IV: We will have one minute of silence to accommodate every child.

Option V: We will refrain from saying the Lord's Prayer, or any prayer for that matter. We will join the Americans in their custom of keeping prayers out of public schools.

After all, public schools are places where children of all creeds meet. It is immoral to violate any child's right to religious freedom.

As educators, we have no right to impose our own religious beliefs on children. We ought to be neutral in religious matters and help children come to their own conclusions of the "truth" logically and rationally.

We have other important tasks to perform, tasks that have nothing to do with prayer. Most of us are not qualified to give religious instruction of any kind. Our role in a democratic society is to help children become good citizens, to develop skills for economic competence and independence, and to encourage children to treat each other fairly and equally.

This kind of justice and fairness, meted out in public schools, has nothing to do with the nature of one's religious beliefs.

All children in our schools should be treated as individuals, with all the rights and privileges accorded to individuals in our society. Religious teaching, worship and prayer have their place in the home and at church, not in the classroom.

Teaching the teachers in Leguan, Guyana

Stop Youth Bashing and Victim Blaming!

By Peter Jailall, The Valleys Sr. P.S.

(*The Beacon*, April 1994)

During the March Break, a gang of youths swarmed a home in Mississauga, overpowered its inhabitants, then took off with money and jewelry.

Another gang in Toronto swarmed a store on Yonge Street, beat the owners, trashed, then robbed the store, leaving one owner with a broken arm.

Across the border, a gang of youths stormed a classroom, stabbed a thirteen-year-old student to death, then terrorized the teacher and students.

There is no doubt that violent crime among young people is on the increase in our society and, as a result, this violent behaviour is played out in our schools. In response, Ontario's Minister of Education has called for "zero tolerance," and the chair of Metro's Boards of Education has embarked on a drive to ban young offenders from school for life.

Manitoba's Justice Minister, Rosemary Vodrey, wants to put children as young as ten years of age in prison for life for violent offenses. The recent federal report on youth violence claims that children as young as six and seven are involved in gang activities— burglary, mugging, assault, and even murder.

Now, violent young adults ought to bear full responsibility for their violent behaviours, and I agree that there must be some penalty or consequence for their criminal actions. But, when children as young as six or seven continue to act violently, then we in the adult community have to look elsewhere to find the causes.

And while it is true that there is an increase in youth violence, the vast majority of our young people are responsible, caring, law-abiding citizens. School administrators and teachers will testify that, in any school, the same small group of students continue to misbehave and act violently day after day, while the silent majority continues to work and behave diligently and decently.

Our youths, though, challenge us to look deeper and harder at the legacy we as adults have bequeathed them. They are living in bad economic times, when all sorts of social and cultural problems surface. Some are turned off school and they know that a good education does not necessarily guarantee a good job anymore.

They have rejected some of our adult morality. They look around and are shocked and confused by the double messages that the greed and vulgar materialism of our sports, political and business leaders demonstrate. At school, young children continue to be influenced by TV and Nintendo. They pick up violence, sexism and racism from computer games and hours of watching television. These negative behaviours are internalized and reproduced in school grounds and shopping malls.

School remains the only meeting place for large groups of young people. They come from diverse racial, cultural and economic backgrounds. Teachers must be fully resourced and supported by all the stakeholders in society to meet the many needs of our modern day school population. As parents and politicians throw up their hands in despair, more and more our task of educating the young shifts from direct teaching to parenting, counseling and social work. We are becoming both teachers and cultural intermediaries as we strive to encourage our students to acquire knowledge and engage productively in associated living.

The heavy-handed approaches of youth bashing and victim blaming are both negative and unproductive. There is no royal road in solving the crises our students face. Growing up is very difficult in today's world. We need all our institutions—the home, the school, the church, the government, business and the media— to work co-operatively to save our youth… our country's most precious resource.

One-to-one instruction during class work

Recipe for a Good Trustee

By Peter Jailall, The Valleys Sr. P.S.
(The Beacon, October 1994)

On November 14th, Peel citizens will be voting for trustees to represent the interests of their children's education. The record of the voter turnout in the past has shown that many taxpayers do not show up to vote, not only for their trustees, but also for their municipal councillors.

But Peel has changed a great deal since the last election—the population has increased and continues to be culturally and economically diverse. The economy is still sluggish and the cost of operating schools has increased. Therefore, taxpayers ought to turn out in large numbers to exercise their franchise, choosing trustees who are informed about the changing trends in education, as well as the complexities of the constituencies. Gone are the days when taxpayers will accept general motherhood educational jargon at the bottom of a candidate's glossy picture.

Mississauga and Brampton, two tiny city nodes sleeping beside the giant city of Toronto, are gradually showing the signs and symptoms of typical big city living—pockets of high-rise, high-density population, poverty, and an influx of new immigrant groups. We are faced with some challenging social and economic problems. The choice of a competent trustee is very crucial during this election. In the past, a few trustees have used their office as stepping stones to Queen's Park and Parliament Hill. On November 14th, the citizens of Peel need to select trustees who will stick around to continue the process of serving their constituencies for the long term benefit of our children. Consequently, trustees are called upon to lay out their platforms clearly and fully.

The good trustee is not just a facilitator who sits quietly during board meetings and votes on issues but one who needs to be committed to the following:

i. That Peel's students become academically competent and successfully challenged in an ever changing world

ii. That Peel's students learn life skills and critical thinking skills

iii. That environmental issues are included in the regular curriculum

iv. That schools have management committees comprising students, parents and teacher representatives

v. That ESL/ESD students are guaranteed full status in the regular classroom

vi. That corporations which benefit a great deal financially from Peel's Education System be willing to pay their fair share

vii. That the "fat" in the system be trimmed by making resource staff and those with administrative duties help in classroom teaching, thus lowering the pupil-teacher ratio

viii. That trustees look at creative ways of helping alienated youth by fostering peacemakers and other apprenticeship-type programs, in partnership with the business community

ix. That trustees look closely at how female students are socialized in schools and how they make progress in mathematics and science

In the area of equity education, here are some questions trustees need to answer:

1. How would you support and extend the equity work done by the Peel Board of Education?
2. What would you do to ensure equity as a major focus in the Common Curriculum?
3. What are your views concerning full employment equity legislation?
4. Would you be prepared to have a survey done on the needs of bright students, ESL/ESD students, lower economic status students and students from ethno-cultural backgrounds?

Trustees do have a very demanding, responsible job during their term of office. Sometimes, the politics of education can become entangled with the pressing needs of children. But, in this period of our Board's history, equity issues are vital—issues that are bound to the democratic process of education in public schools. Trustees need to address equity issues fully if we as educators and leaders are going to prepare the young for living in a truly democratic society.

Voting For Marginalized Students

By Peter Jailall, Queenston Drive P.S.
(The Beacon, October 1992)

Yes! No!—simple words in our language, yet they have become strong political statements these days. Their use on October 26th has the potential of dividing school communities, polarizing provinces and even breaking up the country.

Political, linguistic, native and gender groups are all gearing up for the "yes" or "no" vote during this referendum. Many of these interest groups are well organized with election offices and campaign funds at their disposal. They know how to make full use of their democratic rights, unlike some marginalized students and their parents here in the Region of Peel.

This growing population of voiceless new immigrants and their children are passive spectators amidst this referendum fever. They speak their own language, practise their own culture and religion, and yes they are a very 'distinct' society within the larger Canadian society. I spoke to a few of these immigrant parents about the referendum. They are curious, but they do not seem to understand what the vote is all about. Innocently, one parent said,

"I am new to this country; I do not understand."

They may not understand what the referendum is all about, but they do want their children to learn English in Peel schools. Many came to live in Ontario precisely for that reason. They know the empowerment that proficiency in English can bring. The 'cut backs' are short-changing these ESL learners. More than any other subject, these students need adequate English instruction in order for them to function in their future academic careers. They also need to learn English so that they can adapt socially and culturally to their new country. If they are denied full access to English instruction now, there will be gaps in their academic careers later.

Some of these gaps may never be filled. This will be an unfortunate and sad situation that will be detrimental not only to the future of these citizens, but to other members of society as well.

The little instruction that ESL students receive from classroom teachers is insufficient. How can classroom teachers programme for these students when there are so many other needy ones to teach?

The parents of ESL students completely trust administrators and teachers with the education of their children. How can we betray that trust? We must all be strong advocates for these students. Their parents have no political or linguistic clout like other small vocal groups who can quickly get their wishes by pressing the right buttons and making the loudest noise. As a new people in a new country, new immigrants are afraid and many are confused. They lack the skills of organizing and networking in this vast complex region where traditional organizations are entrenched and even reluctant to include "strangers." They do depend on the goodwill of concerned advocates in education.

The federal government can find millions to spend on this referendum, but it cannot finance the education of immigrant children brought in by its Department of Immigration. Is this all the Ministry of Education and the Peel Board can offer ESL students?

Many teachers and administrators do care about these children's language development and their cultural adjustment in our schools. And when they vote "yes" or "no" on referendum day, they ought to remember the "distinctiveness" of these new comers in their charge whose desire is to learn English.

Working with ESL students in a Grade 8 classroom.
Photo courtesy of the Mississauga News

Farewell

By Peter Jailall, Munden Park P.S.

On June 30, 1998, I retire… and, with my retirement, comes this final chapter of "Jottings." My column began in December 1985, when I returned from a year's sabbatical at the University of British Columbia. After all, elementary teachers are entitled to sabbaticals too! During those earlier times, we were able to apply to the Board for a year's study leave…no more!

Before The Beacon was born, "Jottings" appeared in *The Appeel*, E.A.'s joint publication effort with O.S.S.T.F. District 10.

I would like to thank many people for helping with the final draft and, as the child would say, the "good copy" of "Jottings" over the years. In particular, I wish to thank my friend and colleague Michael Harmer, who has been my writing partner from the beginning. I also wish to thank Rick Taylor for his frequent artistic enhancements of the column. A big thank you to Donna Kinch, who is also retiring in June, for her patience in accepting my late submissions.

Most of all, from the bottom of my heart, I thank those of my colleagues across Peel who took the time to write words of encouragement, words of praise and even strong lines of criticism. I needed that feedback to keep my creative juices flowing. I accept all of your comments, past and present, with an open mind. The criticisms have been crucial for my professional growth, for it's only through constant dialogue and disagreement that we learn. This kind of discourse is essential in preserving our democracy and our system of public education.

I began "Jottings" with a dialogue. Michael and I had many conversations, first in *The Appeel* and later in The Beacon. Through these conversations, in a small way, we attempted to encourage and sometimes challenge teachers to think through classroom practice and other contemporary issues. It was through these conversations between Michael and me that I was able to write "Jottings." For truly, writing is a form of internal and external conversation. Just as I began, 13 years ago in *The Appeel*, I bring "Jottings" to closure with a final conversation with MH:

MH: *After a long, successful and happy career in education, Peter, it must sadden you to leave at a time of such uncertainty and unrest.*

PJ: This year has been stressful and challenging for me, for all teachers. Ever since the protest last fall, things have not been the same in our schools. Teachers are demoralized by the unfair criticism levelled at them. They are overwhelmed by mountains of paperwork and avalanches of curriculum materials.

MH: The Tories would suggest that they are interested only in improving education through fiscal responsibility, accountability and new curricula… where have they gone wrong?

PJ: The Ministry seems to be in such a dreadful hurry! They send down new curricula in June with the expectation that they will be implemented in September. Since the Ministry took full control of education, boards of education have been left out in the cold. Our trustees and senior administrators are struggling with arbitrary directives and inflexible budget lines. This centralization of power has alienated the local school from its own board. Teachers now serve two masters—the Board and the Ministry.

MH: Mr. Harris has played the alienation card with some skill—"money-grubbing" teachers vs. "long-suffering" parents, federation "troops" vs. federation "generals," affiliate vs. affiliate…

PJ: Yes, and now we have the exclusion of school administrators from federation. It has to have an adverse effect on the smooth running of the school, the collegiality. This "divide and conquer" mentality, with all of its political ramifications, is all around us.

MH: Are you leaving a sinking ship? Is there room for optimism in all of this?

PJ: In spite of all the rapid changes, the teacher bashing, the shift in power relations, educators will survive because we are a very resilient bunch. We have a noble history of dedicated service and we are good at practising bypass surgery to deal with threats to our educational health. For most of us, the love of children and the inherent rewards of teaching are enough to keep us going. Despite all the criticism and the technological innovation, as a profession we are irreplaceable. After all the rhetoric, in their sober moments, our critics know that we look after the children. Our detractors don't want our job, couldn't handle it, wouldn't know how.

MH: What will you do in your retirement, Peter? It's difficult to imagine you not involved with teaching children and advocating for teachers.

PJ: I still have some energy and passion left. I'll continue writing, as a journalist and as a poet. I'll continue my graduate work at OISE. I'll be returning to Guyana to continue my volunteer work…and sleep under the coconut tree when I'm tired.

MH: Thanks for everything, my friend. You will be missed.

It's Not Easy

By Peter Jailall
(*Retirement Celebration*, October 23, 1998)

After 33 long years
It's not easy to leave
The Beautiful Garden
Where I've greeted the world
Each morning
At the school gate

After reading little Emma's farewell letter
"Dear Mr. Jailall:
Thank you
For helping me learn things
I will miss you plenty. Good bye."

It's not easy to leave
After the Philistines moved in
Tried to destroy the Beautiful Garden
Served us sour grapes
And rotten apples

It's still not easy
To separate us from Emma

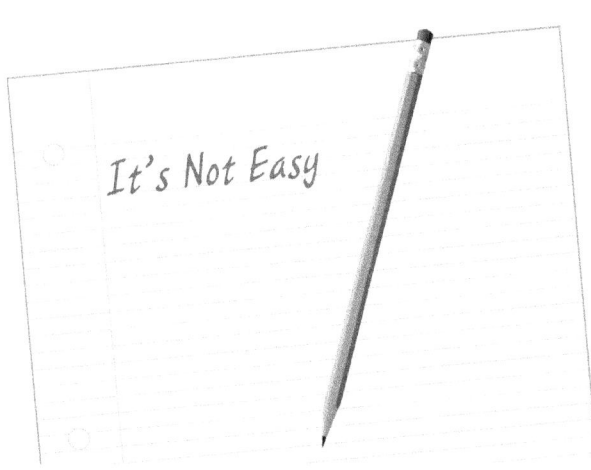

Peter teaching in classroom

Leon Thompson, superintendent of Education, Toronto District School Board, with teachers on the west coast of Demerara

Travelogues

Giving Back

Guyanese Children Living Under a Dictatorship

By Peter Jailall
(August 1990)

"Dalla de lime" "Haversack time" "Scratch time"
These are the voices of suffering Guyanese children shouting above the deafening noise of loud generators along Water Street—generators owned by private business people who provide their own electricity to offset the regular blackouts which descend unannounced upon the city of Georgetown, making this once beautiful "garden city" our own area of darkness.

"Dalla de lime" means three limes for one dollar. Seven year old Trevor Hilton holds up three small, green limes in the palm of his hand, gently clutching them with his tiny fingers to prevent them from falling on the pavement that is always littered with rotten fruit. The buttons on Trevor's tattered shirt are gone and the ends fly behind him as he screams on top of his lungs in competition with the adult hawkers around. He hopes that some passer-by will make a purchase to help him buy a mango for his lunch.

"Haversack sack time" means September is here, the time of year when children are preparing to return to school. The parents of "middle class" children can buy imported haversacks, while poor children go to school like bakers.

"Scratch time" means it is time to take a chance at the local lottery to see if one can win twenty-five thousand Guyana dollars a scratch. Not much mind you, since one Guyana dollar is equivalent to one U.S. cent.

Children Selling, Loitering and Begging

These children are caught up in Guyana's newest ideology—"Hucksterism." They are genuine, honest and hardworking, selling to earn money to buy pencils, exercise books and food to combat the scarcity that has plagued this nation, which is becoming progressively worse each day. They compete with adult sellers in the hustle and bustle of Georgetown's commercial centre giving the on-looker a distinct sense of what it must have sounded like in the tower of babel. Children around restaurants often beg patrons for food or money. How can we blame these innocent children? Their reality is a world surrounded by traders since "trading" has become a way of life which has been imposed upon them by a gang of inept political rulers who have reduced the country to a cap-in-hand state of beggary.

Trading, the imposition of what was once the domain of adults only activities, has replaced play and games, thus robbing children of their childhood, innocence and pleasure. The government sponsored "mass games" with all its military trappings are an order from above that is compulsory and heavy-handed. Children and their parents view "mass games" as punishment, terror and a complete waste of valuable learning time.

Children have become visible street people, trading, begging and loitering in all parts of Georgetown. Young children also hang around ferry boats, mini-buses and airports chasing after people to negotiate a sale or to find menial jobs for which they are paid a measly sum. They have been rushed through their childhood to become "forced-ripe" adults. Whereas in other societies, children are taught the dangers of smoking, along the East Coast road along Enmore, seven-year-old Ramesh sells cigarettes to motorists who stop to pick up passengers. He riffles through the dollar bills with amazing dexterity as he engages in the serious business of negotiating a sale. At Adventure Stelling, eight and nine-year-olds are up at two in the morning selling cheap North American junk brought back by traders. In the rural areas, children also work hard catching fish or shrimps to supplement the family meal or more importantly to sell to supplement the family income. In an adult-like manner, they help with family chores like fetching water from miles away on donkey carts, gathering firewood, cutting grass or watering plants. Many are exploited as cheap labour.

Children Still Creative and Innovative

Children who are not selling, catching fish or working on farms engage in spontaneous play. They have learned to become very innovative. In the absence of foreign technological toys, their creativity and innovation are manifested in their use of local materials to construct their own toys. They use bottle caps to make wheels and pieces of sticks for the body of the car. They work hard to design these toy vehicles without nails which are too expensive or non-existent. As a substitute for nails, they use string to tie parts of their vehicles together. They tie sticks to tin covers to make roller toys. They substitute small rocks for marbles, exchanging rubber bands as payment to the winners of the marble games. Rubber bands can be obtained easily in the society and are used to bundle up wads of Guyana dollars.

Play equipment like climbers and swings are visibly absent in the schoolyard. Manipulatives, sand boxes and clean water, necessary for children to experience the power of play, are also absent in the primary divisions. With no play equipment and manipulatives, children are abandoned to their own devices only to play hide and seek and ring games passed on to them by their ancestors.

In the secondary schools attended by regular students, there is no play equipment like cricket gear or soccer balls, yet students at the President's College are offered horseback riding as a leisure sport.

Children Stranded on the Roads

Children are not only deprived of rich childhood and learning experiences at school, but also experience an ordeal to get there. In the hot morning sun, they stand stranded for hours waiting for transportation. Insensitive, greedy hire car and minibus drivers zoom past these youngsters in preference to adult passengers from whom they can obtain higher fares. The government is helpless. Many state-owned buses are abandoned in a big parking lot in Ruimveldt known as "the graveyard," awaiting spare parts and/or mechanics to service them. Long hours of waiting along the East and West Coast roads result in children experiencing fatigue and frustration on their tedious journey to school. Finally, if they manage to get to school, they are so exhausted and hungry that they are unable to concentrate. Exhaustion, coupled with the depressing environment of the school provide little incentive for learning to take place.

The Barrenness of the Education System

The school buildings are dilapidated—doors, windows, toilets and walls are broken, roofs leak, benches, desks and blackboards are outdated. Children still sit in rows 2 to 5 to each desk. There is no running water in some schools. Domestic animals roam the schoolyards and even inhabit the space beneath the school buildings making the entire surroundings unhealthy and uninviting for everyone. Yet, still occupying a prominent place on the dusty, unpainted walls in schools, are photographs of the late dictator hauntingly staring down at the barrenness, sadness and lethargy that permeate the entire education system.

Tools for writing—pens, pencils, magic markers, crayons, paint brushes and chalk are scarce items. In some schools teachers are required to use no more than three sticks of chalk for the whole term. Textbooks are also a scarcity in the entire country. Parents cannot afford to buy the few that are available in the bookstores. For example, the textbook—Language for Living Book 2, a popular reader used in all elementary schools, costs $745 Guyana.

Reading—An Activity of the Past

The school libraries are empty. The Public Free Library in Georgetown which was once stacked with current periodicals, reference books and magazines is now half full with most of its books being outdated. Computers and photocopiers are sadly lacking. People hardly visit the main library because of its poor collection and blackouts which occur on a daily basis. As a matter of fact, very few people show an interest in reading.

Reading for enjoyment at school and in the society at large is an activity of the past. Young people are not engaged in reading because of the absence of authentic reading material and because there are few adult reading models around them. In some other cultures reading is an essential and enjoyable activity done while travelling or relaxing. During the days of the Guyana Railway Service, readers were in abundance on the trains travelling along the East and West Coast. In Guyana today, the music on the over-crowded minibuses is so deafening that no one can even carry on a sensible conversation. Most Guyanese mothers and their children are so busy "scraping" to get money to buy scarce, expensive food and school clothes that they have no time or inclination to read. The mood of the society—its tenseness, uncertainty, poverty and heavy military rule prevents young citizens from engaging in reading as a leisure activity.

Teacher Shortage and Frustration

Teachers are unable to teach reading in schools because of empty bookshelves. These professionals are frustrated and fed up trying to maintain their sanity in the classrooms under such adverse learning conditions. They complain in vain to the Ministry of Education or to the Guyana Teachers Association while others quit the profession to do trading. Guyana's best teachers have left to teach in the Caribbean, North America and England. Some are enticed to travel to the Bahamas to teach Kindergarten, only to be tricked after they arrive there. Part-time teachers are trying hard to substitute in over-crowded, poorly equipped secondary schools. Some have switched from teaching to administrative responsibilities with other ministries of the government, either to play political games with the party in power or half-heartedly supporting the regime in order to hold on to their top positions.

Like other professions, the teaching profession has collapsed. Except for a few experienced teachers who remain committed, there is no incentive for young graduates to become teachers. Salaries are not attractive enough and working conditions are extremely poor. A trained teacher makes about $1,200 per month (equivalent to $12 US). Some traders make a teacher's monthly salary in one day. No wonder many teachers turn to trading for a living. Those teachers who remain in the profession must be commended for their courage to cope with large class sizes of fifty to seventy students.

At the primary level, Guyanese teachers are just glorified baby-sitters trying to keep children off the streets. Sometimes they are forced to use corporal punishment when they have to break up fights at school.

At the secondary level, there is also a serious shortage of qualified Math and Science teachers. Secondary classrooms have a very limited supply of science textbooks and science equipment. Many secondary students are disappointed, frustrated and angry. Those high school students admitted to the University of Guyana are so poorly prepared academically that they lack basic computation and science skills to cope with the rigorous academic programme.

The curriculum used throughout the Education System from kindergarten to University level is irrelevant to the basic needs of young Guyanese whose minds are too preoccupied with survival strategies—obtaining food and hustling for transportation.

Children Suffering from Constant Fear

Hungry children cannot learn and insecure children are fearful. During periods of long blackouts, children suffer from constant fear. Some are afraid of the dark, while others are afraid of bandits who kick down doors to rob innocent citizens. The very physical structure of homes, schools and offices with iron bars around the windows and doors is symbolic of children imprisoned in the privacy of their own spaces. Children are afraid of police and army men, thinking in their innocent minds that these stern, unfriendly military men are going to lock them up at any time without a reason. Parents transmit a learned culture of quiet submission, helplessness and fear of authority. In turn, children internalize and act out these feelings of inferiority and depression at school. Like their parents, they are afraid to discuss issues, express opinions or to engage in conversations of any kind. Absolute party paramouncy has conditioned these children for twenty-six years.

Like the children and their parents, fearful teachers too have been conditioned to follow orders that come down from the "Big Ones," compelling them to make up numbers during political rallies to impress foreign dignitaries.

School administrators who fail to bring children and teachers out to swell mass rallies are disciplined. Children are used as a means for the narrow political ends of the country's power drunk rulers.

Young people have grown up without any experience of living in a democratic society and Guyanese schools reflect the ideology of a dictatorial system of government.

Children and their mothers continue to be one large group of forgotten citizens who have been taken for granted and ignored by insensitive, intolerable macho leaders at the different levels of government.

Give Children Their Full Rights

Guyana will soon disappear from the map of South America if our leaders continue to deny children their full rights to grow up free from ignorance, fear, hunger and child labour. Nation building is achieved by starting with the children—taking them off the streets, feeding them, clothing them and placing them in schools and playing fields where they can have the full opportunity to grow up as strong, healthy citizens with knowledge, rights and responsibilities.

Children playing in the forest at recess

Going Outside

Teaching without Textbooks

By Peter Jailall

It was my first day working with the British-based project called Guyana Education Access Project (GEAP). I had just finished working with a small group of students preparing them for an interview with the local television station. My job is English Language Teacher Trainer and I was warned by the GEAP head office in Georgetown about the teacher shortage and that the head teachers may want to twist my arm to take over classes without teachers. After a brief discussion in the headteacher's office, he proceeded to take me on a tour of the school. He showed me three different classes in session averaging 30 students per class with young, unqualified teachers teaching them.

"This young man here in room 192 is preparing to write his CXC examinations and he is an unpaid helper teaching this exam class," he confided.

Just before we were preparing to continue our tour of the school, we climbed the stairs to the second floor to room 104. The head teacher stopped and hesitated to enter the room, but suddenly changed his mind. He walked in then greeted the students with his head-teacherly voice.

"Good morning class!"

The whole class of 22 children stood up. "Good morning sir," they replied in unison.

"Do you mean this class has been sitting here without a teacher?" I asked in a puzzled tone of voice.

"These students have been without a teacher since the school year began," the head teacher stated.

"Let's move on to another class," he suggested quietly.

These Form 2 students ages 12 and 13 years in room 104 have been sitting unsupervised, without any instruction all morning since the school year began.

If this were a Canadian classroom the students would all be rowdy. They would be running about the room and out in the corridors getting into mischief and the parents would be up in arms challenging the education authorities.

The principal introduced me as Mr. Jailall, a teacher from "outside" who has come back to teach. I was shocked and also impressed to see a class supervising itself for such a long time. But I also felt a deep sense of sorrow for the students. I could not walk away from them. I looked at them and they looked at me, eyes begging, "teach us, please teach us. Somebody help us."

I could not continue my tour of the school. The moral urge and the obligation to teach them were too strong.

"I'll remain in the classroom to teach these children for the rest of the morning, principal," I said firmly to the head, discontinuing my tour of the school.

He gave me permission to do so as he walked quietly to his office. I turned to the students and said, "Yes, I come from the outside." Without any preparation or lesson plans I used the term "*Outside*" to teach two periods until lunchtime.

"What do Guyanese mean by the term *Outside*?" I asked. Four or five hands went up volunteering answers.

"How many students have a relative *Outside*?" I continued. The whole class put up their hands. "*Outside*" means countries like Canada, England, the U.S. and Barbados," answered one girl from the back of the class.

"Why do Guyanese go *Outside*?" I wrote while posing the question to the class at the same time.

After a lively and humorous discussion both in Standard English and in dialect, I requested that the students work in pairs to continue exploring the question and to come up with answers of their own.

These are some of the answers the students wrote. Alana and Melissa, after a short quiet dialogue proceeded to write:

"People go outside for many reasons. People go for better education, to enter college and some people go for health reasons.

Sometimes your country can't help you so they have to send you 'Outside.' Sometimes you have heart problems or brain damage or problems with your lungs or kidneys. My aunt lives in the USA, she went there for a better job and to be comfortable. My sister and her family went to visit Barbados to see how the country looks like. My grandmother lives in Canada. She sends lots of stuff for me in barrels."

Dennis wrote:

"*My aunt and uncle are outside. They are in America. They send parcels, boxes and barrels for us. It costs a lot of money to go outside. And when they come back to their hometown they dress in the latest fashion and talk deep English. And people go outside to get clear (white skin).*"

Chandia wrote:

"*My uncle sends a small box of toys for me to play with. And my mother sends peppers, mangoes, guavas and lime for them.*"

Dalini wrote:

"*Some people go outside and never return. Some of them also go for trading.*"

Preya wrote:

"Some people may want to go outside because they have family or friends so they know they will take care of them."

The students did not have enough time to write more than one draft, but they took turns to share their writing with the whole class while the others listened attentively. This task gave students an opportunity to improve their reading skills as they practised reading their own text to their classmates. From their writing I pointed out errors in spelling, punctuation, grammar and sentence structure. I used their writing to teach them essential language skills in context. I used their "errors" positively not as criticism for correction only, but as valid information, especially for me, the teacher to teach the necessary skills they needed.

The students wrote for 45 minutes. They were on task; no one walked around the room. They discussed their writing quietly without interrupting others. Meanwhile, I walked around the classroom encouraging reluctant writers, encouraging those who were experiencing writer's block. As I moved around observing students actively engaged in the writing process, I talked about their writing skills as well as the spelling of difficult words and grammatical structures.

The students were dressed in their uniforms with their hair neatly combed. They sat in pairs on wooden benches, the boys sitting separately from the girls. The windows were open and a gentle breeze fanned their faces as they wrote. The classroom was bare, without any books, charts, writing implements or a globe. There was no artwork or children's writing up on the wall. I requested that they read their writing to each other during the last 15 minutes of the second period.

The students handed their writing to me when the bell rang for lunch. No one rushed out of the classroom. Instead, they moved in an orderly manner to go home or to their designated lunchrooms. I said goodbye to the head teacher who invited me to come back soon. Then I headed to the public road to catch a tapir, one of the vehicles that does short drops in the area. Two girls from the teacher-less class had just joined a full tapir in front of me. On the side door of the tapir were the words "Foreign Minded."

"We like to see you tomorrow," one of the girls shouted through the window. She waved goodbye as the tapir, loaded with school children, roared through the heavy traffic, leaving me thinking about the theme *"Outside"* that dominates the lives of people in or outside the school.

Guyana

By Peter Jailall, McBride Avenue PS
(*The Beacon,* September 1987)

Sabi Jailall (Fairview PS) and I spent last August teaching on a sugar plantation in Guyana. With the assistance of generous Peel teachers and students, we gathered stubby pencils, pieces of chalk, used crayons and leftover paper—classroom odds and ends, things that teachers debate whether to throw out or keep for their new class in September.

It was like a kind of homecoming for Sabi and me because we met, got married and taught together twenty-five years ago on this very sugar plantation. When we returned last August, we were teaching many of the children of our ex-students. Parental support was unquestionable. Parents brought their children to class daily and even sat with them at the back of the class during lessons. Also included in the audience were a few of our ex-students who are now teachers in Guyana schools.

We team taught seventy-five students from kindergarten to grade nine. (Class sizes range between 40-50 pupils per teacher). We taught reading, writing, mathematics, drama and art five days per week in the mornings. Classes were conducted in the local dialect and in Standard English.

There were no "discipline" problems. Children and their parents were there because they were eager to learn. Untouched by television or Nintendo, the children listened attentively to Robert Munsch stories. "Love You Forever" was a big hit.

Our school day began with singing some of Guyana's national songs and reciting a universal prayer because of the multi-religious and multicultural nature of Guyanese society. We taught the children "Old McDonald had a Farm," which in turn was taught by them to their siblings at home.

We told old stories—legends and fairy tales indigenous to Guyanese culture. We also told North American stories in Standard English. The children enjoyed the Anancy stories the most. Children wrote daily on whatever topics they chose. We introduced process writing and we found out that Guyanese children, like their Canadian counterparts, always had something to write about. After they had written, their pieces of writing were shared, then mounted on the walls of the old church which housed all classes.

We tried to make the summer program an exciting experience of fun and learning. The children were given a daily snack consisting of a local Guyanese drink and pine tart pastries. After snack time we engaged in a few dances and circle games.

We attempted, in a small way, to bring some joy and happiness to these children, many of whom experience severe difficulties: lack of transportation, scarcity of food and poverty. The schools have no stationery, no textbooks and hardly any chalk. When we left at the end of the program, the children were very happy to receive some of the used pencils, crayons and paper donated by the Peel schools.

We may be returning in August '89, and we are looking forward again to receiving some leftover materials to share with some very unfortunate children.

A lesson in drama with VSO teachers and students

With VSO teacher Tessa

Celebrating World Teachers' Day in Guyana

By Peter Jailall, Munden Park PS

(*The Beacon*, October 1995)

October 5 was World Teachers' Day, a day when we recognize our colleagues from all over the world and celebrate with them our shared task of imparting knowledge and humanizing our global village. Last summer, I had an opportunity to experience global education in all its fullness…

A team of Peel teachers, a retired headmaster from England, a superintendent from the Toronto Board of Education and a high school mathematics teacher from York Region, travelled south to Guyana, the only English speaking country in South America, to work with teachers. The Teacher Education Project was fully supported by the Guyana Consulate in Toronto, as well as by Guyana's Ministry of Education.

During the month of June, we collected paper, pens, chalk and coloured pencils for the Guyanese teachers and children. The Peel Women Teachers' Association donated $500 for books to help in the advancement of literacy in Guyana's schools.

In Guyana we worked at three centres—Leonora, on the West Coast of Demerara, Leguan, an island at the mouth of the Essequibo River and Anna Regina, a small town in the county of Essequibo.

One hundred and fifty teachers, including school administrators, senior teachers and regional education officers, attended our seminars. We introduced the seminars by asking teachers to focus on:

i. Why did you get into teaching?

ii. In one sentence, describe your most passionate belief about education.

We got answers like:

- For the love of children
- To help mould young minds
- With teaching, I have a job to go to
- On becoming a teacher, I became a life-long learner

These are answers we could have anticipated from teachers right here in Peel. It proves that teachers all over the world have a common purpose. Our teaching team conducted workshops in teaching English as a Second

Language, the teaching of mathematics and science, the teaching of reading and classroom management.

The Guyanese teachers were very receptive and participated fully during all the sessions. It was a learning experience both for us and for them. They work under very poor conditions. Classes range between 40 and 60 students per teacher. They lack textbooks and other teaching materials. Qualified teachers earn between $75 and $100 Canadian per month.

The most touching moment for me on the whole trip was when one teacher came up to me asking for a red pencil to mark her students' work. While Guyanese teachers make modest requests for pencils, paper and reading books, their Canadian counterparts ask for expensive computers. We should count our blessings. Working with teachers in another culture can be a worthwhile and valuable experience for teachers in Peel and across Ontario. It's the best kind of professional development a teacher can get. It would be great if, next summer, a few more teachers from Peel volunteer to work with their colleagues in the tropics.

With teacher Suzie from Kamwata School

Working Holiday
By Peter Jailall
(*The Beacon*, October 1996)

No matter where on the globe, teachers face challenges as they attempt to educate the world's children. This has been the experience of members of the Canada-Guyana Teacher Education Project, an organization comprising Canadian and British educators who revisited Guyana this past summer to work with Guyanese colleagues.

We worked for two weeks in two different regions with two groups of school administrators. Principals in Guyana are called headmasters and headmistresses, like their counterparts in Britain. Leon Thompson, team member and Senior Superintendent with the Toronto Board of Education, discussed the topic Education, Leadership and Team Building. He talked about the head teacher as curriculum leader, responsible for the professional development of teachers in the school.

Sabi Jailall (Fairview P.S.) led a seminar on the teaching of English as a Second Language. In Guyana, people speak a dialect of English—also called the Guyanese language—but they use Standard English in its written form to communicate officially in the workplace.

Judaman Seecoomar, a retired headmaster from England, conducted a seminar on the teaching of reading. I addressed the issue of whole language teaching for the development of whole persons.

The majority of the administrators with whom we worked are headmistresses. They are very competent, experienced and knowledgeable with respect to teaching and learning. They demonstrated a real willingness to learn and share their ideas with us. They talked about the limitations that make life and teaching difficult in a developing country: lack of funding, poverty, the scarcity of textbooks and science equipment. The headmistresses said that they would like to see more trained teachers enter the profession to replace all the veteran staff members who have emigrated to teach in other countries. We discussed the management of children's learning: the acknowledgement of learning as an outcome of children's interest, the guidance of children in managing their own language and the maintenance of classroom order and discipline. The Guyanese classroom is open concept, an experiment we tried here in the sixties by physically breaking down walls to make our classrooms open. The openness of the Guyanese classroom makes it a fertile ground for team teaching and integrated learning.

Our intention was to continue to build collegiality with our Guyanese colleagues, share ideas with them and learn from them. We left some books, stationery and teaching aids, and promised to return next summer. One valuable lesson we learned from the Guyanese educators was the value of willingness, patience and perseverance when working in adverse conditions. For most of them teaching is not a job…it's a calling.

With Region 7 teacher Pam

With VSO UK teacher Ian

Learning from the Natural Environment

Peter Jailall, advocate for rural education and development, uses local resources to help push learning in the hinterland

(*Guyana Times*, October 2011)

Peter Jailall described as a teacher, poet, storyteller and an avid supporter of human rights, education, social justice and environmental protection, volunteers with the Canadian University Service Overseas (CUSO-VSO), as a teacher-trainer in Guyana. In 2010, he received the Guyana Cultural Association Education award for his work in rural education and community development in Guyana. His published books include "*This Healing Place*" (1993), "*Yet Another Home*" (1997) and "*When September Comes*" (2003).

Two weeks ago, Peter Jailall, Ian Funnel, Shelly Dickson and Katie O'Donnell, all volunteers, visited the community of Region Seven, where they conducted workshops and training sessions with teachers and learning programmes with students, who hailed mainly from Amerindian communities.

His most recent visit last week was to Kato in the Pakaraimas in Region Eight.

He described both visits as very successful and refreshing, and thanked all the other volunteers who participated, as well as students and teachers who were very friendly and cooperative.

He recalled his trips to Regions Seven and Eight in an interview with *Guyana Times Sunday Magazine*.

Recollections

Last week, the VSO team worked in Kato, a small Amerindian village on the Pakaraima Mountains. The people there speak Patamona and Guyanese dialect.

Very young children walk two to three miles to school every day. They come from all directions to school, walking along the "walking trails"—a pathway that was carved out by their ancestors many, many years ago.

"I assisted the children attending Kato Primary School to make texts based on their own natural environment and from their own experiences. Their world outside the school is a large science laboratory easily available and ready to be used in the teaching and observation of science. We worked together to create this poem," he said.

Down the Walking Trail

I walk down the walking trail
And what do I see?
I see a big brown baboon
Smiling at me

I walk down the walking trail
And what do I see?
I see a black monkey
Trying to bite me

I walk down the walking trail
And what do I see?
I see a large green iguana
Blinking at me

"Using poetic forms, I encouraged the children to utilize the setting around Kato to describe the life of their pet cat, thus making their own text familiar to their natural setting. Reading texts from their own environment becomes more meaningful than reading about snow and big apartment buildings in New York or Toronto," he noted.

Jailall told stories to the whole school during assembly, and conducted a workshop with all the teachers. He also taught science and literacy to grades two and five with VSO Raquel Cohelo and Lennox Boston, literacy coordinator in Mahdia.

The children enjoyed the rhythm and cadence of the language as they participated fully in reading, writing, science and art. The VSO teaching team, as well as the administrators in Kato, worked hard to bring closure to the theme, "Transforming Guyana through Science and Technology."

Meanwhile, a group of teachers in Region Seven worked closely with students at St. Anthony Primary School in Bartica, Itaballo Primary School and Agatash Primary School, to assist in teaching science through literacy.

The first text used was "The Great Kapok Tree" by Lynne Cherry, a book about the different species of animals that live in the rainforest of Guyana. "Turtle, Turtle Watch Out!" by April Pulley Sayre, was the second text used which follows the dangerous journey made by a leatherback turtle at sea.

After exploring the texts and using drama and choral reading to develop ideas, the children created their own writings, either about preserving the natural habitats of the rainforest or about a turtle's life cycle.

During oral discussions, the children used the Guyanese Creolese to describe life in the rainforest from personal experiences. For example, "The jaguar de de deh as she wait for food along the food chain." (The jaguar is there waiting patiently for food along the food chain). Another example was, "Turtle, she hatch she eggs p'an Shell Beach." (Turtle hatched her eggs on Shell Beach). They then translated these ideas into Standard English.

Each of the children will have a piece of their written work included in a published book which will be displayed in Guyana and taken back to Canada and the United Kingdom.

"I look forward to working with our children again," Peter declared.

With VSO teacher Anna from Holland

With head teacher Eula from Moruca

Children of Mabaruma

By Peter Jailall
(*News Update: Canada-Guyana Teacher Education Project,* October 2007)

We are children
Of the radiant sun
The fertile rain
The refreshing wind

We are friends
Of green parrots screeching
In the sunset
Of wild ducks dashing
In the rain
Of yellow butterflies floating
In the wind

We are friends
Of buzzing bees
Making honey in the trees
Of wild deer
Nibbling cassava leaves

We are friends of howling monkeys
Jumping and swinging with ease
Of sunfish diving
Gliding down swift waterfalls

We are friends
Of lazy alligators
Tanning on river banks
And of big turtles
Hatching on Shell Beach

We are children
Living on the edge
Of the rainforest
Children of Mabaruma
In beautiful Guyana

Reflections on Volunteering Three Weeks in Mabaruma, Guyana

By Peter Jailall

I left the poem entitled "Children of Mabaruma" behind and in return, I took away their gentle, innocent smiles that I will cherish for a long time. A relaxed, peaceful way of life is etched on their beautiful faces and they are calm and gentle in school, causing no visible discipline problems. These children, poor in material things, make their own toys from scraps of wood, pieces of fine rope and discarded small wheels. They fish, catch crabs, hunt for birds and small animals and they climb tall trees to pick fruits.

They walk long distances to school, paddle canoes, swim across deep rivers with ease and they even imitate the sounds of nature. They know their terrain well, and at times I watched in awe as they interacted so harmoniously with their natural environment.

Often, I reflected upon the instructional approach I could utilize to address their educational needs. I still continue to think about this, since teaching these children and helping their teachers teach them continues to pose a challenge to me. Teaching materials are in short supply and there is a shortage of trained teachers. I was told by one teacher that each classroom is given a sheet of bristol board and a box of magic markers per term. Young children, though, need many fat markers to write instead of skinny lead pencils. Fat markers help to strengthen and develop their fine motor coordination. Paintbrushes and lots of colourful paint are also an asset.

I went as a member of the Canada-Guyana Teacher Education Project (CGTEP), a diaspora organization based in Mississauga, Canada, in partnership with VSO Canada and VSO Guyana. This was a pilot project funded by CIDA. I was sent to Mabaruma (Region 1) as a Volunteer Teacher Mentor. I found the VSO staff to be very friendly and helpful.

I arrived in Mabaruma on Monday, September 17th, 2007 after an uneventful plane ride, which lasted approximately one hour. I reported to the Regional Education Officer, who assigned the assistant Education Officer to take me to visit Mabaruma Primary School. On my way to the school, I met two VSO teachers from England. We had a lot in common regarding our philosophy in education and we immediately established a professional bond.

I was interested in a grade 9 class called "Primary Tops" by the education authorities, so I spent some time with the classroom teacher teaching these needy students. We engaged in conversation about their lives and as a follow up activity, composed a piece of writing together with its setting in Mabaruma. It is entitled *The Mabaruma Alphabet*.

During my short stay at Mabaruma Primary, I worked with the teacher-librarian, writing stories with her grade 4 children and teaching them to read. I discussed the possibility of helping to improve the sparse collection of books in the library. I also did a workshop on "Language and Literacy" with the whole staff at that school. The Head Teacher was very supportive. She dismissed the school one hour early to give me an opportunity to extend the afternoon sessions with the teachers. After each workshop, teachers asked questions about reading, writing and the local dialect. They requested that I do a follow up workshop with them when I return in January, 2008.

At the request of the Head Teacher at Horsororo Primary School, I told the grade 2 students a story. My story was relevant to the animals and folklore of the culture. I donated a set of science books to the Science Department. Also, in that school, I did a creative writing lesson with a National Volunteer who had just arrived that day to teach there. Horsororo Nursery is across the road from the Primary School. I taught the nursery children a song and told them a story.

With the assistance of an educational consultant, I visited Shell Beach on the weekend. Two Canadian filmmakers assigned by VSO-Canada, came along to interview the National Volunteers on the trip.

On Shell Beach, we met with the captain of the Shell Beach Community. He is a local conservationist who is very knowledgeable about the habitat of turtles. He informed us that the big leatherback turtles, an endangered species, come out at night to lay their eggs in the sand. He made a request for some VSO teachers to give their services to the Almond Beach Primary School, which is located on Shell Beach.

Already, I miss the children of Mabaruma. They call me "the funny, friendly ole man," a term of endearment. I promised them and their teachers that I would return to tell more stories and recite more poems and do more workshops. We planned to teach and do a training session both in Mabaruma and in the town of Bartica in September 2008.

> "I took away their gentle, innocent smiles that I will cherish for a long time."

Teaching in Guyana

By Peter Jailall, The Valleys Sr. PS

(*The Beacon*, August 1991)

Recently, the Peel Women Teachers' Association generously donated $500 worth of books to help a literacy project in Guyana. Five Peel teachers, together with three others from the Greater Toronto area, will be going to Guyana in August to work with a group of Guyanese teachers in the county of Essequibo. Peel teachers have been visiting Guyana regularly over the past eight years to work with students and teachers during the summer months.

In August, this team of teachers will be conducting literacy lessons focusing on reading and writing. We will be using the textbooks donated by the Peel Women Teachers' Association to help us in the project.

The presence of Peel teachers in Guyana this summer is a significant gesture in building collegial relationships between our systems. The Peel teachers on the project are expatriate Guyanese who have been working in Peel for a long time. Some of us also have experience working in the Guyanese school system. We are going to learn from the teachers there, as well as share ideas about teaching and learning. We are very aware of and sensitive to the cultural and linguistic needs of the students and teachers there and members of our team are knowledgeable in the teaching of English as a Second Language. When we return, we hope to be available to share our ideas and experiences with Peel teachers to help their program meet the needs of new students from Guyana and other parts of the Caribbean region. The need for teacher education in Guyana is vital. The education system collapsed under the previous regime and now educators, both in Guyana and abroad, are working to rebuild the system. We would like to thank publicly the Peel Women Teachers' Association for its gift and those people in Peel who have helped us in the past. We thank Larry Baswick, Mike Harmer, Ernie Keuchmeister, Paul Shaw and Judy Caulfield for their continued support. Also, we make an open appeal to educators in Peel during this clean-up month of June. Consider us for any used supplies. We do not need books. Please send your donations to Sabi Jailall (Fairview PS), Aruna Gayadeen (The Valleys Sr. PS) or Jennifer Chin (Trelawny PS). Again, thanks for your support and have a safe and enjoyable summer.

Guyana's Future Stunted by Shortage of Trained Teachers

By Peter Jailall

(*Indo Caribbean World*, July 5, 1995)

Meet three Guyanese students who joined my class at the beginning of this school year.

Jane is from Buxton Village on the East Coast of Demerara. She attended Buxton Community High School before she came to live with her father in Mississauga. This is her story.

"I lived with my mother in Buxton and I visited the Annandale Market regularly. I also visited my relative in Beterverwagting. In my class there were 40 students, and used to sit on the back bench."

"We did not have enough text books, so the teachers used to copy the work on the blackboard. Sometimes it was hard to see from so far, so I did not write anything."

"When the rain fell, we did not go to school because the place was too muddy. And our school leaked in many places."

Jane felt comfortable talking to me because I am also from Guyana, but she was very reluctant to speak in front of the whole class.

At the beginning of the school year, last September, she was unable to read simple storybooks. But as the year progressed, I helped her improve her reading skills. She borrowed books regularly from the classroom library to take home. At the end of June, Jane was able to read short novels comfortably.

Like reading, her writing skills—spelling, punctuation, and grammar improved significantly over the school year.

The second student, Neville, comes from Rosignol, Berbice. This is his story.

"I attended Rosignol High School. Me and my friends used to shoot birds and catch fish by the Berbice River. Sometimes, we used to skulk from school. When we go late to school, the teacher does beat us."

"I like this school because the teachers here don't beat. I like TV, the malls, and the video games."

I gave Neville a pencil, an eraser, a ruler, and a box of crayons when he started out on his first day. "Do I have to pay you for this?" he wanted to know. "No," I replied, "but you will have to take good care of them."

Like Jane, Neville at first experienced great difficulty reading and writing.

As a result of his inadequacy in language skills, he was unable to read instructions to do science experiments and to solve mathematical problems.

But by May, Neville started to show improvement in language. Then he started to make progress in all other areas of the curriculum, even though he still remained shy to speak in front of his peers.

The third student, Donna, arrived in December from St. Mary's School in Georgetown. She spoke in her Georgetown accent. This is her story.

"Sometimes we does go down to the public library to borrow books and magazines. We even spend time studying in the library."

"The Minister of Education even came one time to encourage us to study hard."

"In Georgetown, we get to read a lot of books, magazines, and newspapers. We watch television and listen to talk shows."

Unlike Jane and Neville from the countryside, Donna came to my class a very literate student. Her writing had voice and a sense of audience. Her spelling was accurate and her punctuation appropriate.

Donna was not afraid to express her views in class, and she was also proud of her Georgetown accent. Before the school year ended, she was at the top of her class.

Maybe growing up in Georgetown exposes students to literacy activities in libraries, bookstores, the theatre guild, television and radio stations, more than in rural areas.

In spite of the limited experiences of Jane and Neville, instruction and exposure to a literate environment bring out the best in them. Most of our children coming out of Guyana are bright, willing and ready to learn.

Unfortunately, they are victims of a political system which underdeveloped a whole generation. The physical conditions of many schools in Guyana are not conducive to learning— overcrowded classrooms, together with the absence of textbooks and equipment.

Most importantly, there is a shortage of trained teachers. Many of them left the system because of victimization, or to escape the oppression of the People's National Congress regime.

Teachers in any society are the backbone to economic, social, and cultural development. We need a rigorous teacher-education program to raise the level of literacy in order to restore humanity in Guyanese society. Our children are our country's future.

Educator Urges Ongoing Training for Teachers – Impressed with Hinterland Children

By Oluatoyin Alleyne
(*Stabroek News*, April 1, 2012)

A well-known Guyanese educator and poet is advocating continual classroom training for teachers as a means of improving the country's education system, since teachers are the foot soldiers of the system and if they are not good at what they do then the system will fail.

"Our teachers are not trained on the ground. I am not talking about Cyril Potter College of Education (CPCE). I am talking about in-service, in-house training in the school," Peter Jailall said in a recent interview with the *Sunday Stabroek*.

Jailall, who has over 42 years of teaching experience in Guyana, Canada and the US, said it is important for there to be an ongoing process of learning for teachers instead of them just being trained at CPCE.

"Education is a lifelong process and teachers have to be trained to be lifelong learners themselves so that they can inculcate in children this idea of lifelong learning.

He said for teachers to feel they have "arrived" after college is "nonsense" and not good enough.

"We need informed teachers, teachers who are constantly encouraged, supervised and taught how to teach."

Stressing that it is not a criticism of the country's teachers, Jailall said the teachers need support from the authorities and should be provided with books and materials so they can do the job.

An advocate for good teacher education, Jailall sees it as very important in the interior and across the country because teachers are the ones who mould the nation adding that he is "very passionate" about the issue.

"Because our children are our real resources, our rich resources, not only the mineral and the oil and the gold…the future of this country will depend on the children and how we educate them."

Additionally Jailall said the future of democracy in Guyana stems from a very literate, educated population.

In recent times Jailall, who has been back to Guyana every year since 1985, has spent time teaching at the Wallaba, Karaburi and Kamwatta primary schools in Kato, Mahdia, Mabaruma and Moruca.

He works for the Canadian University Service Overseas (CUSO) and in collaboration with the Ministry of Education has been working in many schools around the country since 1998. But recently his focus has been on working in the interior, and Jailall said he is fascinated with the nature of the students in those areas coupled with the richness of the environment. He uses the environment to teach the children science and to create topics for writing that are relevant to their lives

He doesn't only teach the children, but their teachers also, and has been using the Guyanese proverb, "Far a pah mek ochro dry a tree," to describe the state of education in the interior and what happens far away from the coastland and the centre of Georgetown.

"Just how ochro gets hard and dry and spoilt when not reaped on time because they are far away, the same may happen to children attending school in the hinterland if they are neglected and not properly taught," he said.

The educator said local persons from the hinterland communities need to be trained to become teachers as teachers from the coastland would not want to go into those areas to teach.

"You have to train the teachers who are there—to meet the needs of students in hinterland."

'Mash up'

And the educator told the *Sunday Stabroek* that he has been using Guyanese Creolese to 'mash up' Standard English.

Describing Guyanese Creolese as "sweet" Jailall said he always uses this before teaching the children Standard English.

Jailall is of the opinion that using Creolese language in the classroom is a more effective way of teaching children, especially those at the primary level. Usually, Creolese is not encouraged in schools and according to Jailall it is seen as a "bad language."

"But I showed them as an example of how Creolese can be used to teach standard English. And by mashing up the language…means I dissect the language; I translate it and at the same time use it to teach Standard English effectively," he said.

The Creole is part of the children's "soul" the educator said, and it is difficult to keep it away from them, so instead they should be taught to keep the Standard English in their "back pockets and pull it out when it is necessary…"

The very theatrical Jailall said that he is very excited about this form of teaching and he has already seen how effective it is by the difference in the manner the children responded when he first entered the school and by the time he was ready to leave. He said Guyana's Creolese has all the elements of what a language is— verb, subject agreement and rhythm—and should not be "run down" but used effectively.

"For example I will tell the children a story and they would use their own terms to describe the story," Jailall said.

He gave the example of a story about an annoying fly, where one child wrote: "The fly in the story prappa badaration," the educator wrote what the child had written in large letters on the blackboard then a translation into standard English "The fly is very annoying."

To motivate the children to write, Jailall said, he asked them to take him on the path they travel to school and after having a discussion with them about what they see during their journey, he started a poem and told them to continue it.

"I asked the children about the wildlife, the flora and the fauna in the area, we talked about it and we wrote about it…" he said.

Jailall is also a poet and a storyteller and he brings all of this to the classroom where he describes himself as a "performance teacher" with the aim of holding the children's interest.

"I have been coming back since 1985 because I love Guyana, it is my home and I love the children and I want to impart some of the knowledge I have in my own country," he told the *Sunday Stabroek*.

He works with teachers and students and he encourages the children to write. Their written work is shared and placed in the learning centres for children to read in the afternoons.

"Children making their own texts—it is not a new idea but for here it might be a new idea—and teachers as writers…because you cannot teach writing if you don't know to write yourself, so teachers have to learn to write themselves," he said.

But he is impressed by some of the writing of the children and gave the example of one girl—Arita Benjamin—who was very descriptive when she wrote about two jaguars entering her yard and killing two pet dogs. (see text box).

According to Jailall, his experience teaching the children in Regions 1, 7 and 8 is that they can read, write and process information and are extremely knowledgeable about their own environment. He said while the results at the national examinations from these regions may not be as good as other regions, it is because the children are not properly taught.

The "texts" made by the children will be in their own words about their interests and they are not only learning to write and read but also they learn some science. By using the children's vocabulary to teach them Jailall said it will be more interesting and effective than textbooks talking of things the children never experienced.

Wallaba Primary School. Moruca, region #1
Arita Benjamin, grade 8
Thursday March 15th, 2012

When Two Tigers Killed our Dogs

Ever since they were puppies, I fed them and played with them. I loved them dearly. Their names were Brownie and Donkey.

Last Saturday night two tigers with black and brown spots on their coats came to our yard at 12 o'clock. The dogs began to cry: "ow, ow, owwww." They were terrified of the tigers who roamed in the big bush nearby.

Immediately, my dad Vadan armed with his sharp cutlass rushed out of the house to see what was the matter. My mother shouted: "Vadan, kill those tigers now!" My dad yelled: "Hey tigers, go away! Get out a de yard right now, leave dem dogs alone!"

But it was too late.

The bigger tiger had already killed Donkey and the smaller tiger was pulling away Brownie by the neck into the bush. Blood was squirting and pitching everywhere. Both tigers disappeared into the bush with Brownie, leaving a trail of blood.

I went to bed, sad and scared. I did not sleep well, all night grieving for my two pet dogs. Next morning my auntie Eve came over to sympathize with us.

"Those same tigers killed my dog Blackie last week," she reported angrily.

Donkey's body was still on the grass, her body badly mangled with teeth marks all over her belly.

My dad dug a deep grave and buried Donkey in our backyard behind the coconut tree. We never found any trace of Brownie again. The two tigers are still lurking somewhere in the big bush not too far from our school while the whole village is on alert. "Whose dog will be next?" I wonder.

Arita's story was corrected and edited by teacher Peter Jailall from CUSO International, who was teaching at Wallaba Primary School during the month of March 2012.

Teaching in Bartica

We, the CUSO Team, wanted to demonstrate that the writing process could provide an opportunity for closure for the pupils after the Massacre of February 17th 2008.

Politicians, Church leaders and Community Leaders visited Bartica to comfort the adults. We, the members of the CUSO team, attempted to bring closure to the children by using poetry, drama and writing. We used the poem "The Gentle Giant" by Toronto poet Dennis Lee, to prompt and stimulate children's writing.

The teachers in St. John the Baptist Primary School were teaching letter writing at the time. So we requested that the students write letters to the Gentle Giant expressing their feelings about the Massacre.

Here are some of the students' letters:

St. John-the-Baptist Primary School Second Avenue
Bartica 2009-03-06

Dear Gentle Giant,
How are you? As for me I am fine, thank you.
There was a very bad thing that happened in Bartica at the stelling on 17th February 2008 at 9 o'clock. I heard the bullets of the guns on that day, I was very scared on that day. My mother went to see her best friend Edwin Drakes. I was scared when she told me that she had heard when the gun shots were going pow! pow!—she was very scared at that time. She thought it was firecrackers. Then my grandmother said that it was not firecrackers—it was gun shots. That night we were watching cricket and then we heard it. I started to tremble and my mother said, 'Don't scream.' It was the scariest thing I ever heard about, but I hope it will not happen again for ever. I hope it will not happen in this new year.
Your friend,
Kelly Fitzpatrick

Dear Gentle Giant,
How are you? As for me I am fine. But there was shooting on the stelling and innocent people got killed. The bandits came in a boat and bullets were licking. I was wondering what was happening as I was watching the television. I was traumatised and I went to my bed and my mother called me out of the

bed and she said, 'Let's go under the bed!'

The soldiers came to have a shoot out. The bandits went to the Police Station and killed innocent people. In Bartica we saw that bloodshed on the Monday. I did not go to school. My mother said that I could go to school on Tuesday. Blood shed on the stelling and people got shot.

Your friend,
Keshon Benjamin

Dear Gentle Giant,

How are you? As for my family and me, we are going fine, but, Gentle Giant, there have been terrible things happening last year. There was a massacre; gunmen or bandits were shooting all over the place. The bandits came in a green boat and innocent people got gunned down by gunmen. My mother was looking at the cricket on the television when it was happening and she woke us up. We were scared, and we need peace and love in Bartica. I want them to stop this, Gentle Giant. I was sleeping when my mother told me, and I saw some blood. It was horrible. It is a bad thing to do. The gunmen shot the guard, innocent people!! I am sorry about that. I saw a man in a freezer with blood—he got shot. That man at Banks, he got shot down, too. I am sad about that.

But what goes around comes around. Your friend,
Odella

Dear Gentle Giant,

How are you? As for me I am fine. Thank you. I am just writing this letter to tell you about the massacre that was happening on February 17th that was last year. 12 civilians were slaughtered on that day. They were on the street and I was watching television with my mother and brother—my dad was in the bush working. When we were watching television we heard gunshots. 12 people were killed, 3 police, 1 guard, 8 people too. The gunmen were shooting all around the community in Bartica and on the next day the twelve people were shown on television. Most people were traumatised, even me was traumatised and what made me more sad were the people's loved ones crying. I'll never forget that massacre, what happened on that day I never thought that a massacre like that could happen in Bartica. I thought this was a peace place in Bartica, so that is all I have to tell you.

Your friend,
Kishaun Tracy

Dear Gentle Giant,

Long, long ago there a massacre happened with plenty of guns in Bartica. I was sleeping but after I heard it I woke up and heard gunshots and I was scared. In the morning blood was over the road, 3 men died at the stelling and 3 policemen died in Bartica. That was bad. They rode everywhere. I saw a bandit shot a policeman and after his phone was ringing. We saw blood on front Street and there were so many bodies in Bartica. That was the first time it had happened and they killed innocent people. Six people died in a boat and one jumped out of the boat and swam away and the gunmen did not know that. The gunmen then took the police van and put their guns in it.

Your friend, Kezia

Dear Gentle Giant,

How are you? I am sending this letter to tell you about what happened last year in Bartica. It was a massacre. Everyone was scared. They shot the policemen and one of Vulture's guards, one by Citizen Bank and many more on the road. There was a gang of them. Everyone was wondering about their family when they were on the road when the massacre was going on. They came in a green boat and they shot 6 men at the stelling. Everyone was watching cricket while the massacre was going on; one person was shot in his car, people were hiding in the trench.

The soldiers were searching all over. They went in the line too. Some people were hiding underneath the bed. Every morning the police and the soldiers were searching everywhere in Bartica.

Your friend,
Colin Timmermann

Dear Gentle Giant,

A bad thing happened at the massacre in Bartica. You should have seen it. It was 10 men brought up in a green boat.

All the people ran to see the people who got shot. They got shot in their head, gentle Giant! That was very horrible. I was scared. There was blood in the green boat. I turned to my mother and said; 'Mother, you see how people die!' I was sad. Because why? One was a driver. It was one of my mother's friends. When my mother heard that, my mother jumped out of the chair. My mother's heart began to beat fast, too fast.

Everyone say that they carried the dead people to the mortuary and put them in the freezer.

I was in bed and when I got up I saw my mother crying coming back.

When she came she told me what had happened.

When I saw that she was crying I felt so sad. The next morning I did not come to school because I was afraid.

Tamika John

Dear Gentle Giant,

Last year bad things happened. Gunmen came to shoot people up. They came in a green boat. Bad things happened in Bartica. They shot the police and they called the President. He came. He brought soldiers to carry the dead people to the hospital. The people felt sad and they cried.

My grandfather prayed. He said, 'Please God don't let bad things happen to us.' I ran under the bed I was afraid. I cried when I saw men with a hole in their face and blood coming out. They killed the fat man who was looking at the cricket. All over his body. I was frightened to go to school in Bartica. We want to live in peace. We do not want bandits to come here. Paul a policeman ran under the bed and my sister said, 'Is a man shooting his own wife?' My mother thought it was squibs.

Next morning when I woke up it was a sad thing in Bartica. I went in the shop to see the dead on television and when I saw the dead I was crying.

Shania Thorn

Dear Gentle Giant,

I hope you are fine. I am writing this letter to tell you all about last year. What horrible things happened last year! The people were so scared. The bandits came and shot them and robbed them. The police tried to come but the bandits shot the police. Things happened when the people were asleep. The gunshots woke us up from our sleep. People went to look out the window and the bandits shot her. Her son ran outside and hid. All the people cried for their mother and father. They were so scared. They think they would get killed too. The bandits wanted money. The mother and father hadn't any money to give to the bandits and so they killed the man and all his children and his family. The people were so scared that they ran away. Last year it happened so fast. It was too much of trouble for us. It was guns shooting and people ran for their lives. It was so horrible a thing.

So I am happy for you to come back to live with us today. I was so happy to tell you what happened last year. It was so horrible that day.

Your friend,
Sue-Ann Liverpool

Dear Gentle Giant,

Bad things happened last year with gunmen. It was a horrible thing. I was scared. They shot policemen up. They stole their money, the bandits robbed the bank. They came in a green boat that night. It was so terrible I couldn't sleep. I was scared. They came at eleven o'clock in the night; they attacked the police station, they killed them out.

I was afraid to go to school. The bandits never came back to Bartica.
Your friend, Orwin

With students of Bartica

With colleague Judaman Seecoomar at the Santa Rosa monument, Guyana

Using the Guyanese Language (Creolese) to teach Standard English

The Lives of Children and the Language They Use in the Community

As a new teacher in the community surrounding the schools where I taught, I spent the first week visiting homes from which the students came. These visits were intended to observe how the students lived, examine their language habits and their cultural values, then follow them into their classrooms. There I would be better informed to teach them and conduct on the spot training sessions for teachers "because the teacher's relationships with those he teaches cannot be sustained in a vacuum. The homes and the neighbourhoods of the children must remain a part of their life when they come into school – which means that we cannot afford to have schools that stand aloof in the community they serve (Britton, 1979, p. 188)." I listened and joined in the conversations with the students and their parents. I speak and write the Guyanese dialect fluently.

Creolese, a dialect of English, was the spoken mode. Developing over two centuries, Creolese in Guyana has become a fully developed language "as complete in every way as other languages" (Fromkin & Rodman, p. 263). Guyanese from all social classes use Creolese in its spoken mode, while Standard English is always used in schools, businesses, politics and commerce particularly in its written form.

In this predominantly East Indian community in the upper Corentyne Berbice, children and their parents speak a particular variety of Creolese that differs from other varieties spoken in cities or villages in Guyana. This Berbice variety of Creolese is punctuated with a greater amount of Hindi – the language brought from India over 170 years ago by indentured labourers. I listened and recorded a conversation between an Indo-Guyanese mother, Indra, and her daughter Gallo who lived on Middle Street where I also lived. The Standard English translations are in brackets.

Indra: A haad aze yu haad aze gal, yu pasray deh. Me a tak to yu ova an ova an yu na a move. Me pull out yu eat and you na even badda wid me.

(Are you really that stubborn, girl? You sit there so comfortably. I am speaking to you over and over again and you are not moving. I dished out your dinner and you are completely ignoring me)

Gallo (8 years old): Me a cum. Wait na, maye.

(Gallo is dipping and pouring water from a tub using the halves of a coconut shell as containers) (I am coming, Mom. Please wait)

Indra: Hey Gallo! Watch me. Watch me, na gal. Yu bittle gu ge cole. Dis homan na move. She prapa baad. Heh eh! Me gu ge yu sum hat lash in yu behine.

(Hey Gallo. Look at me in the eyes when I'm speaking to you. Please look at me, girl. Your food is getting cold. This young lady refuses to move. She behaves badly. Oh, my dear. Oh, my dear. I am going to spank you on your buttocks)

Gallo: Me a cum jis now. Wait nuh!

(I am coming in a minute. Please wait)

Indra: If me pick wan whip me gu mek dis homan sid donk wan place.

(If you do not move promptly, I'm going to break a whip from the trees and compel you to sit in one place as I whip you all over your body)

Gallo: Me a cum now, maye.

(I am coming right now, mother)

Indra: (Running toward Gallo with a whip and uttering threats at the same time) Aye gal, yu maad. Yu na a hear wen me taak to you? (She raises the whip over her head threatening, but Gallo runs in the kitchen to eat her dinner)

(Hey girl. Are you crazy? Are you not listening when I am speaking to you?)

In speaking with her daughter, Indra used the word 'pasray,' derived from Hindi meaning "to sit comfortably in a very relaxed disposition. It is a word that is used frequently in Region X and in many other regions in the country. The statement "me pull out yu eat" is a version of Creolese used specifically in Region X. It means: "I have dished out your dinner." Indra expressed an adjective of degree when she said, "she prapa bad" meaning she behaves very badly. This description of bad behaviour or 'stubbornness' is used extensively at home and at school, both by parents and teachers. Interestingly, the word "bittle" has survived since the days of British colonialism in the country. It was derived from 'victual.'

A few houses away from where Gallo and her mother lived, Sankar, a cane-cutter and his son Avinash (14 years old) were sitting on a small bridge leading into their yard. I spoke to the father and son. The son had dropped out of school. First, I spoke to Sankar who normally is head of the household and most qualified to talk about matters concerning school:

Peter: Sankar, tell me wha mek yu son lef' school. (Sankar, tell me, why did your son leave school?)

Sankar: Teecha, dis baye ya na wan fu gu back a school. Hole day e deh home an sleep. He seh dat e hate school. Wen e git up, ya gu ketch bird and fish. E a walk about al day.

(Teacher, this boy does not want to go back to school. All day he stays at home sleeping. He tells me that he hates school. As soon as he wakes up in the mornings, he goes to catch birds and fish. He walks about all day)

Peter: (Addressing Sankar's teenage son) *Wha mek yu na want fu gu a school, baye?* (Why don't you want to go to school, boy?)

Sankar: Teecha, it cas too much money fu sen dis baye a school. Me caan afford fu buy book and clothes fu send am a school. (Teacher, it's too expensive for me to send this boy to school. I cannot afford to buy books and school clothes)

Avinash: Hole day ahbe a waste time a school. Ahbe na a du nuthen. School too borin'. (All day we just idly sit at school. We don't do any work. School is very boring)

Peter: So wha yu gu du when yu grow up? (So, what are you going to do when you get older?)

Sankar: Me wan Avinash fu gu "Outside" in America whey e gu get wan good edication. Dis place na gat fewcha fu me son. Me muma live in New York an she put in fu me already. Me done get fuss paper. A soon as me get am, me gaan. All me ga fu get a somebody fu look afta me house. (I would like Avinash to go to America where he is going to get a very good education. This place (Guyana) has no future for my son. My mother lives in New York and she has already sponsored me. I got my first letter (from the Immigration Authorities). As soon as I get (the rest of my papers) I'm leaving. All I need is someone to take care of my house).

Like many parents in the community. Sankar sees a very dim future for his teenage son's education but he is too poor to support him at the local school. His son, too, is not enjoying school and as he claims, he is "wasting time" and school is "too boring." Like Avinash, there are many teenagers who have dropped out of school. Not only in Region 10, but in the whole of Guyana, the dropout rate is alarming.

At age fifteen, school attendance ceases to be compulsory. "From age eleven, the percentage of children enrolled in school diminishes, varying considerably between types of school and, with increasing age, it varies with gender also, as girls are more likely to attend school and succeed" (Adult and Non-Formal Education in Guyana, March 1999, p.9). At Line Path Government School, the enrollment reveals 327 girls and 205 boys in attendance in October 1999.

Teenage boys who have dropped out of school and are unemployed "hang out" on bridges and kokers – sluices that were installed by the Dutch *(After the Napoleonic Wars, the Dutch colonies of Essequibo, Demerara and Berbice were ceded to Britain in 1814. In 1831, they were united under one administration in British Guiana. At independence in 1966, British Guiana was renamed Guyana)* during colonial times to regulate the flow of water into the Atlantic Ocean. Some of these teenagers sit on the beach and in rum shops for hours. In the community surrounding School A, teenagers do part-time jobs unloading "smuggle boats" that bring in contraband, toiletries, dry goods and clothes from the neighbouring Dutch country of Suriname. Some teenagers work as conductors on mini-buses and tapirs – the locally assembled cars. Thirteen-year old Mohan is engaged in a sales activity which Berbicians call "walk and sell." He walks slowly along Middle Street, his head covered with a bundle of coconut brooms shouting, "Brooms for sale!"

On Baptist Church Street, girls as young as 13 years old drop out of school to stay at home. I spoke to Sattie – 14 years old – who dropped out of school:

Peter: Why you leave school at foteen years? (Why did you leave school at age 14?)

Sattie: Me daddy tell me fu cum out a school fu laan sewing. At school, dem baye a trouble me al de time. (My father told me to leave school and take up sewing lessons. At school, the boys used to bother me all the time)

Peter: Wha you does do at home wen yu sewing class done? (What do you do at home after sewing classes are over?)

Sattie: Me does help me muma do housewuk. Like sweeping de yard, washing wares and cooking. Den me does listen to music. (I help my mother do housework like sweeping the yard, washing dishes and cooking. Then I listen to music)

Peter: Wha yu gu do wen you get older? (What are you going to do when you get older?)

Sattie: Well, me daddy gu look wan baye fu me marry. Fix me up wid wan baye from Canada, nuh? (Well, my father will look for a young man for me to marry. Can't you fix me up with a young man from Canada?)

Many of the teenage girls like Sattie who dropped out of school are engaged in domestic chores at home, helping their mother sweep the yard, fetch water and doing most of the cooking for the family. East Indian girls socialize differently from the teenage boys in the community. They are not permitted to walk outside late at night except when accompanied by adults. Most of them are housebound, listening to music or watching American T.V. In cities and small towns, businessmen run Nintendo Clubs where school children hang out. Many 'play hookey' as the Canadians would say, or 'skulk' from school as the Guyanese would say. On April 2nd, 2000, the Guyana Chronicle Newspaper reported that "police caught 53 primary and secondary school students in Nintendo clubs when they should have been in school. They were found on March 1st, 2000 and on March 3rd, 2000 in separate raids on five Nintendo clubs in the capital city of Georgetown. One child among the lot never attended school.

I selected a poem from one of my poetry books written in dialect *This Healing Place (1993)*:

<u>Baan Fu Wuk</u>

"I man, coolie man
Baan fu wuk
Cut bush
Bruk dutty
Wet me haan
Wid white saliva

I man, coolie man
Baan fu wuk
Plaan rice
Cut rice
Fetch rice
Soak me toe
Wid mud wata

I man, coolie man
Baan fu wuk
Plaan cane
Cut cane
Fetcha cane
Soak me haan
Wid sal wata

I man, coolie man
Baan fu wuk
Plaan Bhaji
Cut Bhaji
Sell Bhaji
Soak me skin
Wid drain wata

I man, coolie man
Baan fu wuk
Wuk
An me wuk
Wuk
An me wuk
'Til wuk fricken me."

This poem addresses the theme of work, of growing crops familiar to the students' own environment. It is written in the students' own voice reflecting their cultural and linguistic experiences.

I wrote the poem on the board, then asked students to read it quietly without verbalizing. I observed that they read their dialect with ease. Afterwards, I read the poem while they listened. Students were asked to read the poem individually and then with a partner. From my observation of the students' participation, they enjoyed reading the text; phonetically, they "called out" words that were not familiar to them. They enjoyed the rhythm of the language and the repetition of words in the poem. They made the text their own. At the end of the lesson about five students were able to repeat lines from the poem from memory. It was clear that they derived some pleasure from reading the text written in dialect. Some of the students took copies of the poem home to read to their parents and grandparents. Taking the scripts home enables them to share the text with their families and at the same time, encouraged reading activities at home. As a follow up writing activity, students were asked to write the poem in Standard English. Ryan wrote:

"I am a coolie man
I am working since I was born
I work and I work
Until work is afraid of me."

Rita and Sylvie working as partners wrote in their translation of the second verse:

"I am an East Indian man
Since I was born I was working
I cut bush
I burn bush
I dig up dutty
I wet my hand with spit
To give me grip."

These two students extended the Creole words of the poem using other words in Standard English to make meaning.

Nizam and Gobin, two boys, worked together to translate the second verse of the poem:

"I am a hardworking man
I plant rice
I cut rice
I fetch rice
My toe is always soaking
In muddy water."

Ramesh, who wanted to work alone, translated verse three:
"I working since I born
I plant cane
I cut cane
I fetch cane
My hands are sore
Then I soak them in salt water."
Anil and Ramu translated the fourth verse of the poem:
"I am a coolieman
I work in the garden
I plant callaloo
I cut callaloo
I sell callaloo
My skin get wet
When I fetch water from the drainer."

The students were eager to work alone and in small groups to translate the poem that they understood very well because it related to their everyday experiences working, planting and reaping in their kitchen gardens and farms.

After the translation from dialect to Standard English, students read their versions individually and collectively. They asked each other and the teachers present for the spelling of difficult words and they proofread to determine the placement of correct punctuation marks. This activity validated the students' use of their own language. The transition from 'dialect to standard English' gave them an opportunity to make a "connection between the language that they already know and use to the language (standard English) they need to learn, in order to communicate in speech and in writing at school and in the business world."

My use of poetry written in dialect opened up new horizons for the students: the validation of their own language in print. I ventured to use their dialect as a vehicle to teach Standard English even though dialect is not fully encouraged or sanctioned by the designers of the Ministry's curriculum guides and even by many teachers and school administrators. The students, though, were very keen in using their own language. From the positive experience gained by the use of the poem written in dialect, "Baan Fu Wuk," I was encouraged to pursue some more language learning activities taken out of the students' own "everyday talk." My aim was to combine reading with oral language and sentence construction. Further, I encouraged the students to describe events in their everyday life. The following sentences were selected and put on the board:
"Me bin a Skeldon market fe by."

"*Me bin a rice feel gu wuk.*"
"*Me bin a punt trench fu swim.*"

At the end of the lesson, sentences written in dialect were juxtaposed with translations into Standard English which students were able to read on the board:

"*Me bin a rice feel gu wuk*" – I went to the rice field to work.
"*Me bin a Skeldon market fe by*" – I went to Skeldon market to buy.
"*Me bin a wataside fu pray*" – I went to the waterside to pray.

Further, the students, their teacher and I ventured to explore positive, comparative and superlative using dialect. I wrote on the board:

"*Dis bai bad.*"
"*Dis bai bad, bad.*"
"*Dis bai bad so till…*"

Students were requested to translate the above in their exercise books. Parpattie wrote:

This boy is bad.
This boy is very bad.
This boy is very, very bad.

The students in the class worked together to explore the word 'dem:'
"*Dem gaan a "Merica.*"
"*Dem fambly sen wan barrel fe dem.*"

Roy's translation read:
"They have gone to America."
"Their family sent a barrel for them."

For homework I asked students to record a conversation with members of their family, then translate the conversation into Standard English. The following is a sample of Hera's homework which was done as he collaborated with his mother at home:

Ma:	Hey sum money
	Gu a shap
	An by sum goods
	Fe me na bai
Hera:	Hu much goods yu want, ma?
Ma:	Me wan two pung aloo
	Wan battle cooking hile
	An wan gallan rice
Hera:	Ge me de money, quick ma.
	Me hurry
Ma:	Cum back quick, bai
	Na play, play a road cana
Hera:	Aright, ma.

For homework, Hera wrote this conversation between himself and his mother in Standard English:

Ma: Here is a sum of money.
Go to the shop and buy some groceries, please, my son.
Hera: How much groceries do you want, ma?
Ma: I want two pounds of potatoes, one bottle of cooking oil and one gallon of rice.
Hera: Give me some money quickly, ma. I'm in a hurry.
Ma: Come back quickly, boy. Don't play by the roadside.
Hera: Alright, ma.

I wrote this dialogue in dialect between Hera and his mother on the board. Some of the students laughed in amazement to see their own home language brought to life in the classroom. Then we worked together as a class to translate Hera's homework. In the process of translation, we explored the word "quick" both from Hera's and his mother's utterances. I pointed out the use of the adverb "quickly" in this example.

Hera: Give me the money **quickly**, ma.
Ma: Come back **quickly**.

We discussed at length the meaning of the two words play, play repeated. I wrote the children's different renditions of "Na play, play a road cana." Sylvie offered:

"Don't play play corner the road."
Gaitree: "Na play a the road cana."
Ryan: "Don't play by the edge of the road."
Geeta: "Don't play by the side of the road."
Mohan: "Don't play on the parapet."

As a class, we explored different ways of translating the dialogue – the use of apostrophes and contractions (i.e. do not = don't). We arrived at different meanings of the Creolese word *cana*:

Cana = corner of the road:
Road corner;
By the edge of the road;
By the side of the road;
On the parapet'

I demonstrated step by step the different meanings that we could extrapolate from their own speech. In this exercise they were engaged in reading, grammar instruction and expanding their vocabularies both in Creolese and in Standard English. The students' interest in this process of language teaching was very high. It was very clear that they were making full use of their own language to explore Standard English.

I encouraged high school students to write freely in their own dialect.

Thelma, a student in Form 3 wrote:
> Every aftanoon afta school
> Me does sid donk pan me veeranda
> An wan bai dos pass
> An e dos watch me "cut eye, cut eye"
> Til wan day
> E write me wan letta
> E sey how e love me bad, bad
> An how e can walk
> Wan thousand miles fu win me heart.

Thelma shared her poem with the whole class and other classes in the school. She even read it to a wider audience using the medium of the local television in Region 10 and parents were delighted to hear their own language – Guyanese dialect, spoken on television by one of the younger members of the community.

Meena, a parent in the neighbourhood, saw and heard Thelma's poetry reading on the television. The next day she told me:

Me like hear ahbe dese own talk on T.V. How me laugh! Da gal poem mek me remember far. She mek me remember ahbe own Guyana T.V. show, "Agree to Disagree."

(I like to hear our own language on T.V. I laughed. That girl's poem made me reminisce. Her poem brought back memories of our own Guyana T.V. show, "Agree to Disagree.")

"Agree to Disagree" was a popular local Guyanese talk show in the late 1990s with characters using dialect as the dominant form of communication. Many students like Thelma have the knowledge and the ability to use dialect as a powerful mode of written expression if only their teachers and school administrators would refrain from categorizing dialect as a debased form of English. More so, if teachers could see the merit and possibilities that the use of the children's mother tongue can bring about in language and learning, they will capitalize on its usefulness in the teaching of Standard English. Deep meanings and significant idioms emerge out of the Guyanese language. For example, when I explored the meaning of "Cut eye, Cut eye" in Thelma's poem, with the whole class, students were asked to explain the term:

Angie: *"Cut eye Cut eye" mean when you like somebody and your parents don't want you to see dat bai, so you give dem dat look underneath so nobody else can see you.* ("Cut eye, Cut eye" means when you like someone that your parents don't approve of. So you give that look underneath (when no one is watching) so nobody can see you.)

Buddy: *"Cut eye, Cut eye" also mean when yu get angry wid somebody and* you get so angry you don't want fe talk to dem." (Cut eye, Cut eye" also means when you get angry with somebody to the point where you don't want to talk to them)

Kasilla: Me does watch me muma cut eye, cut eye when she na 'gree fu sen me to party at night. (I shoot quick glances at my mother when she doesn't agree to send me to parties at night).

The Guyanese idiom of "cut eye, cut eye," generated a lively discussion leading the class to explore important cultural and societal values facing youths in the Berbice area.

I encouraged students in teacher Rajpaul's class to choose their own topics for writing. Afaz wrote about celebrating his birthday with a group of friends:

One day at April 28 was my birthday. I selerite my birthday and I invityed my friends. I was happy wid the presents my frend broth. I invity my nebers and all my cozens to come. We all have nice time my prepered some nice tings. My mom tek out fotograf. After my friends went to the Cinama to see a film name, "Eye for an Eye."

As a regular practice, teacher Rajpaul marks a piece of writing with a red pen, underlining all the errors in spelling, punctuation and grammar. He then asked the students to rewrite compositions after assigning a low mark. I brought to the teacher's attention Afaz's natural use of dialect in the above piece and suggested the translation of these words into Standard English using the format of a mini lesson. I also suggested that students be given an opportunity to talk about their writing intentions before and during the act of writing so that they could generate important ideas to write about. By doing this, they might be in a better position to write more vigorously because they would be choosing topics based on their own experiences. Afaz's experience, like many other Guyanese students, is the celebration of a birthday after which he and his friends went to watch a movie at the local cinema. Experiences like birthday celebrations, playing cricket, going fishing and hunting are pleasurable pastimes for Guyanese young people. Teachers would be wise to capitalize on these pastimes for classroom discussions as well as writing opportunities. The Guyanese teachers recognize the importance of children writing with partners or in small teams, in an atmosphere free from fear of criticism or error making.

In a Form II classroom, I used the text *Do Not Open* because the story is set near the sea in Region 10. Students are knowledge and have real experiences about life near the sea. Before I read the story, we talked about the lives of people who reside near the seashore. I asked the question, "What are some of the things people find at the seashore?" One student answered, "driftwood," and another said "bottles or shells."

I read the story to the class, then asked students to rewrite the story in their own words. During the process of writing, students were told to ask for the spelling of difficult words they may need during their writing. In the absence of dictionaries, I wrote the words from the story to assist the students in their writing.

Students were requested to write the story *Do Not Open* in their own words. This is Dianand's story:

<u>Do Not Open</u>

Miss Moody live by the Water Side alone. Everyday, wen the water washed, Miss Moody went with her wheelbarrow to see what she could find. The first time wen Miss Moody went out, she found a wit cat. The cat was sick. Miss Moody pick up the wit cat and put it in the wheelbarrow and walk home and Miss Moody give the cat some milk to drink. Next morning wen Miss Moody wake up she take her wheel barrow and den she found a clock and she take home the clock and put some oil den the clock start to wuk and stop work. Den the next morning she went out to see what she can fine, den she fine a bedsheet. Den de storm start she fine a bottle with a mark do not open and wen she open the bottle a baccoo come out de bottle. Miss Moody sed I do not scare of you only a scare of mouse. Quickly the baccoo turn into a mouse and Miss moody cat skmbr the mouse. Aftr Miss Moody never open bottle a gaind.

I read Dianand's story to the whole class because he was too shy to read it. Afterwards, a few students volunteered to read their stories. As I conferred with Dianand, I pointed out some errors in spelling, like 'den' and 'de' storm. These spelling errors are very common among students because they write the words based on their pronunciation. They all omit the 'th' sound in words. For example, students commonly spell 'then', 'there' and 'these' as 'den', 'dere' and 'dese', respectively. I pointed out to the classroom teachers that Dianand and his classmates should be given an opportunity to make these errors in writing and that these errors should be used in teaching vocabulary, pronunciation and spelling skills. Dianand and his classmates should also be given opportunities to write freely, and dialect words that appear in their writing should be translated into Standard English. But most teachers are very reluctant to encourage students to give voice to their writing and to accept any form of Creolese in its written mode. Yet they use it all the time in speech to instruct students and to converse outside of the school. I made use of the students' writing using their scripts as an opportunity to teach Standard English. Here are some examples of dialect words taken out of their written assignments:

De – of, (out of)
Wen – when

Den – then
Wite – white
Trou way – throw away
Wuk – work
Sed – said
Fine – find
Friken – frightened

In a Form 4 classroom, I introduced a poem written in Guyanese dialect – *Ahbe Dese and Dem da* – taken from my book of poetry *This Healing Place and Other Poems*. I wrote the poem on the board and read it to the whole class, and then I asked students to quietly read it to themselves and translate it into Standard English. This is Farouk's translation (in italics):

Ahbe dese a Christian	– We are Christians
Demda a heeden	– They are sinners
Ahbe dese a high naysian	– We are high class
Demda a begga	– They are beggars
Ahbe dese gat rum shap	– We have a rum shop
Dem live haan to mouth	– They are poor
Ahbe dese bin ya fus	– We were here first
Dem cum afta	– They came after
Al yu cum from de country	– You come from the country side
Demda a patak	– They are nothing

After the children completed their translation of the poem, they shared their writing with others in the class. Then we worked together, translating the Creolese into Standard English:

Ahbe dese = we
Bin = were
Ya = here

We also talked about an alternate translation for some words. The students enjoyed translating their spoken home and play language into Standard English. They also gained confidence using their own language and they were delighted to see their own oral language in written form.

From my early experience as a teacher in Guyana's classrooms and later as a teacher trainer in the schools of Region 10, I observed a practice of teacher-centred teaching, especially in the areas of Language and Literacy. Jamaican-born educator, Dr. Zellynne Jennings (2000) described this practice as teaching that "is typified in the banking concept of education in which the teacher gives, the students receive, the teachers tell, the students listen; the teachers give notes, the children copy them." In all areas of language teaching I observed in schools, teachers were engaged in this "teacher-directed method." I agree with Dr. Jennings' proposal of a progressive method of instruction that can be applied to language teaching and learning. Her proposal exposes some flaws in this "teacher-centred" way of teaching – teacher talk dominating students' oral participation, students passively copying teachers' notes from the black board, teachers engaging students only in the mechanics of language teaching.

Dr. Jennings challenged Guyanese teachers by suggesting, "Progressives tell us that something is wrong with this way when it is the only way and should be corrected by making teaching student-centred as well. Let the students discover knowledge for themselves. In this way, (they) will be more independent to accept more responsibility for their own learning."

In the absence of texts – including children's literature – novel sets and poetry books, I propose that teachers make full use of the resources present among the children – their stories and their own language. The aim ought to be for students to be competent in code switching and become confident in accepting the appropriateness of "register" when the occasion arises. I further suggest that teachers use the richness of the language and culture already present in the community surrounding the schools. In the absence of storybooks, I introduced (with modifications) some children's literature I used in Canadian classrooms to the Guyanese teachers and their students. I demonstrated how literature could be used effectively in the classrooms to teach language skills. I also showed how the dialect used by the students could be incorporated to teach Standard English through translation. The students enjoyed the process of translating their own language into Standard English. The teachers observing did not object after they saw students taking responsibility for their own learning as they experimented with the dialect.

It seems to me that the students were revealing to the teachers how creative and exciting it could be to explore the dialect and Standard English together.

In light of the above and in contrast to what has gone on before, what follows are recommendations regarding an appropriate approach to a Language and Literacy curriculum and instruction for Guyanese schools together with a program of teacher development:

- Teachers need to validate the Guyanese dialect as an authentic language and not as a debased form of English in schools.
- Teachers should be encouraged to use the home language of the students and their parents as a base to teach Standard English.
- Teachers should use oral language to teach Standard English and to explore other forms of knowledge across the curriculum in the absence of books in the schools and in the society at large.
- Teachers and students need to explore storytelling as an integral part of the language curriculum. Students will benefit in vocabulary building in

acquiring Standard English and in developing self-concepts.
- Parents and grandparents should be encouraged to tell stories relating to Guyanese culture and history to their children and grandchildren.
- Teachers and school administrators need to continue modelling Standard English in their speech during classroom instruction and other school related activities.
- The Parent-Teachers' Association needs to seek financial assistance from local businesses to help in the purchase of books and stationery.
- The Parent-Teachers' Association has a role to set up libraries in the schools for both school and community use.
- Guyanese teachers need to work closely and in partnership with teachers from CIDA, GEAP and other NGOs.
- The Ministry of Education should collaborate with all headmasters and teachers to focus on a national literacy campaign.

Santa Rosa Primary School, Guyana

Books by Peter Jailall

Children like to write
Omnipress, 1983

Improve Language Instruction
Omnipress, 1984

When September Comes
Natural Heritage/Natural History, 2003

Yet Another Home
Natural Heritage/Natural History, 1997

This Healing Place and Other Poems
Natural Heritage/Natural History, 1993

Mother Earth: Poems for Her Children
In Our Words Inc., 2009

Sacrifice: Poems on the Indian Arrival in Guyana
In Our Words Inc., 2010

Jottings—a Teacher's Logbook
In Our Words Inc., 2014

www.ingramcontent.com/pod-product-compliance
Ingram Content Group UK Ltd.
Pitfield, Milton Keynes, MK11 3LW, UK
UKHW021310180426
11947UKWH00015B/1140